Trout, Salmon and the Evening Rise

The Barometric Breakthrough

By

Andrew Bett

To Paul,

With very best wishes for your
next fishing expedition !

Andrew Bett

COVER PICTURE: Campbell's Run on the Amat Estate water of the River Carron. A watery sun breaks
through after rain in Glen Carron; wonderful weather for fishing.

Photo by Allan Donaldson

Published by
Salar Pursuits Ltd
P.O Box 117
Heathfield
East Sussex
TN21 1AF

info@salarpursuits.co.uk

Designed by **Malcolm Wilson**, Horsmonden, Kent
Printed by **Print Wells**, Tunbridge Wells, Kent

ISBN 0-9552418-0-4

Dedicated to Colette, and to the next generation of Bett fishers; Harry, Alastair and Eleanor.

Introduction

This book seeks to find the hitherto elusive answers as to why salmon take a fly in fresh water, and what it is that stimulates feeding activity in trout, sea trout and salmon (either actually, or as a conditioned reflex). The intention is to describe how a theory about salmon behaviour in fresh water led to amazing empirical evidence that formed the basis for a seven year study. The findings of the study are supported and confirmed by many years of zoological research, not yet seen or published within the world of game fishing. The study into salmon behaviour also examines scientific research that provides a new understanding of the responses of aquatic insects, and therefore also of the feeding habits of trout and sea trout.

I have been very fortunate in receiving help, advice and encouragement from the most senior biological researchers in the UK. I would like to thank Dr Peter Fraser of Aberdeen University Zoology Department, Dr John Blaxter of Dunstaffnage Marine Research Laboratory in Oban, Dr Peter Barnard and Steve Brooks of The Natural History Museum Entomology Department, London, Dr Peter Hunt of The Shellfish Association of Gt. Britain, based in the Fishmongers Hall, London, and The Freshwater Biological Association, Lake Windermere, Cumbria. The conclusions of the research in this book would not have been possible without their donation of many years of study work, publications and experience, the use of which they have generously permitted.

Contents

To Spring

O thou, with dewy locks, who lookest down
Thro' the clear windows of the morning; turn
Thine angel eyes upon our western isle,
Which in full choir hails thy approach, O Spring!

The hills tell each other, and the list'ning
Vallies hear; all our longing eyes are turned
Up to thy bright pavilions: issue forth,
And let thy holy feet visit our clime.

Come o'er the eastern hills, and let our winds
Kiss thy perfumed garments; let us taste
Thy morn and evening breath; scatter thy pearls
Upon our love-sick land that mourns for thee.

O deck her forth with thy fair fingers; pour
Thy soft kisses on her bosom; and put
Thy golden crown upon her languish'd head,
Whose modest tresses were bound up for thee!

POETICAL SKETCHES 1783

William Blake

Chapter One

The generations before us

'A merciful providence fashioned us hollow,
on purpose that we might our principles swallow.'
H.W. Tilman

So many wonderful books have been written about trout, sea trout and salmon fishing, by the greatest exponents of these differing arts, it is hard to imagine that anything further can be added. Thankfully fishing books will continue to be written if only for the simple reason that days spent fishing are unequalled in peace, contemplation, friendship and pleasure. Fishers will continue to write – just for the fun of it. But books down through the ages all add something to the sum of knowledge, since they all contain the important ingredient of experience, and it is the sum of experience that I have so far gleaned from the great gurus of fishing, past and present, from fishing friends and from ghillies that has led to the writing of this modest contribution. In fishing nothing is absolute, and the theories and conclusions of this book are only another small step on the road to a better understanding of the behaviour of trout, sea trout and salmon in our rivers and lakes.

A day out fishing is an almost indefinably wonderful experience, and perhaps Lord Grey (later Lord Grey, Foreign Secretary 1905-1916), in his book 'Fly fishing' 1899, comes close to capturing the essence:

'Often after walking a mile or two on the way to the river, at a brisk pace, there comes upon one a feeling of 'fitness', of being made of nothing but health and strength so perfect, that life need have no other end but to enjoy them. It is as though till that moment one had breathed with only a part of one's lungs, and as though now for the first time the whole lungs were filling with air. The pure act of breathing at such times seems glorious. People talk of being a child of nature, and moments such as these are the times when it is possible to feel so; to know

the full joy of animal life - to desire nothing beyond. There are times when I have stood still for joy of it all, on my way through the wild freedom of a highland moor and felt the wind, and looked upon the mountains and water and light and sky, till I felt conscious only of the strength of a mighty current of life, which swept away all consciousness of self, and made me a part of all I beheld.'

At the same time as these words were written, my great great uncle was thoroughly enjoying a countryman's life of hunting, shooting and fishing. He was particularly fond of salmon fishing on the magnificent Tay river in Perthshire, Scotland and would send fresh salmon in a basket down to his niece, my grandmother, in Cambridge on the overnight train. His huge 18 ft bamboo and split cane rods are still with us, as well as enormous salmon reels loaded with hundreds of yards of greased silk line and backing. We also have some of his salmon flies – great meat-hooks dressed in the familiar patterns of the day; Mar Lodge, Hairy Mary, Thunder and Lightning and Jock Scott. He must have enjoyed harling on the Tay, as we have some

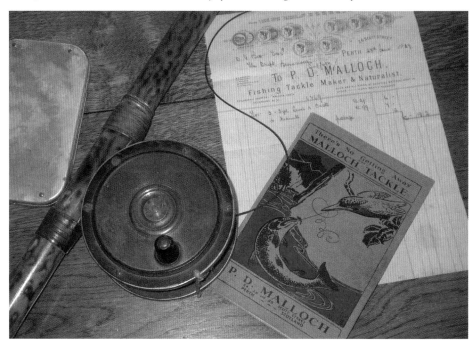

The rod, fly box, reel and greased silk line that belonged to my great, great uncle; and a 1939 copy of 'P.D Mallochs' Fishing Tackle', together with an order from my great grandfather, dated the same year, for three yard casts and a few minnow mounts – no doubt of the variety that slew the 64 lb cock salmon for Miss Ballantine on the Tay in 1922.

of his evil looking minnow mounts; and I wonder, also, what he would have made of the huge catches of the post war period. Perhaps the spinning minnow mounts that we have were bought from Malloch's of Perth, who famously supplied the minnow mount and line that Miss Ballantine used to catch the biggest salmon ever caught in British waters in October 1922; a 64 lb cock fish from the Glendelvine water of the River Tay. Perhaps great great uncle Fordy actually saw the brute on display in Malloch's window! Not to mention Mrs Morrison's 61 lb cock salmon, caught on a fly (the biggest British salmon taken on a fly) not two years later from the Lower Shaw Pool of the Deveron.

The period between the two world wars was a golden era for salmon and sea trout fishing in Britain. Fishing equipment and techniques were greatly advanced, and from what we read of contemporary fishing accounts, the knowledge and understanding of salmon and sea trout behaviour was every bit as developed and informed as you might expect at a time when fishing parties were catching literally hundreds of salmon in a week and Highland and country estates were employing ghillies and guides for a lifetime's dedicated service. One can expect these ghillies to have been highly experienced, seeing many, many hundreds of salmon and sea trout caught each year and in all types of water and weather conditions. The added knowledge of the habits and behaviour of salmon and sea trout of those days has been passed down through the generations and forms, of course, a large part of our knowledge today. But, thankfully, when it comes to fishing it is each to his or her own, and when advice is offered we can take it or leave it. Since fishing for trout, sea trout and salmon is far from an exact science, the approach and the techniques are simply a matter of opinion and of choice. But there's one thing all fishers have in common – we all want to catch fish, and if someone has discovered a new trick that actually works then most people will give it a try, since it never hurts to try something new, and even old dogs can learn new tricks!

FOLLOWING PAGES: Traditional salmon flies and lures from my great grandfather David Bett's 1934 Hardy's catalogue. By kind permission of Hardy & Greys Ltd, Alnwick.

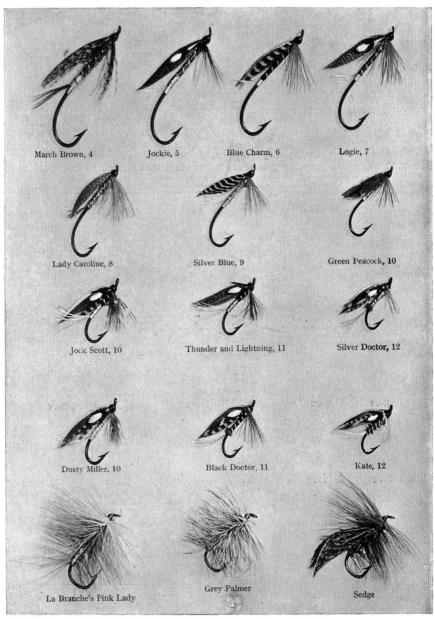

March Brown, 4   Jockie, 5   Blue Charm, 6   Logie, 7

Lady Caroline, 8   Silver Blue, 9   Green Peacock, 10

Jock Scott, 10   Thunder and Lightning, 11   Silver Doctor, 12

Dusty Miller, 10   Black Doctor, 11   Kate, 12

La Branche's Pink Lady   Grey Palmer   Sedge

LOW WATER AND EXTRA SMALL SALMON FLIES AND
SALMON DRY FLIES. PLATE 8.

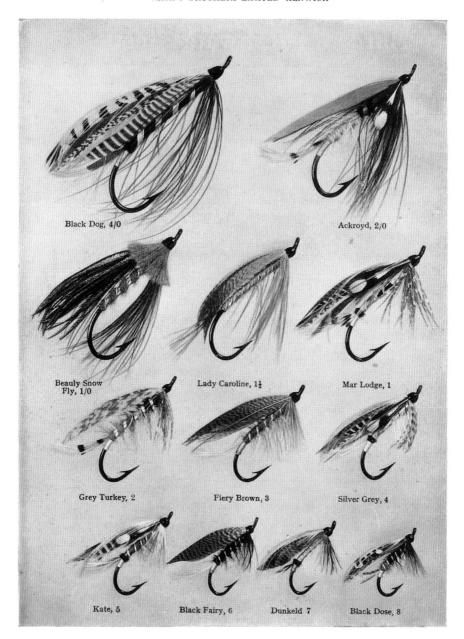

Black Dog, 4/0

Ackroyd, 2/0

Beauly Snow
Fly, 1/0

Lady Caroline, 1½

Mar Lodge, 1

Grey Turkey, 2

Fiery Brown, 3

Silver Grey, 4

Kate, 5

Black Fairy, 6

Dunkeld 7

Black Dose, 8

GENERAL SALMON FLIES. PLATE 12
ON HARDY'S OVAL WIRE-EYED HOOKS

No. 6/0, Black Ranger

No. 1/0, Wilkinson

No. 5/0, Murdoch

No. 1½, Red Drummond

No. 4/0, Red Sandy

No. 2, Black Dose

No. 3/0, Bull Dog

No. 5, Seabrook

HARDY'S AARO SALMON FLY WITH SPINNER.   PLATE 13

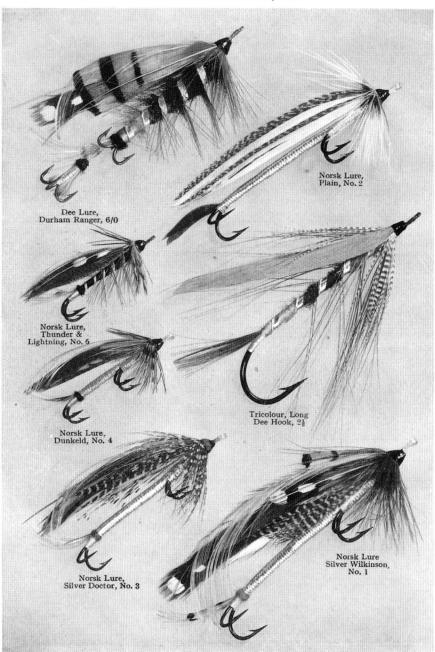

Dee Lure,
Durham Ranger, 6/0

Norsk Lure,
Plain, No. 2

Norsk Lure,
Thunder &
Lightning, No. 6

Norsk Lure,
Dunkeld, No. 4

Tricolour, Long
Dee Hook, 2½

Norsk Lure,
Silver Doctor, No. 3

Norsk Lure
Silver Wilkinson,
No. 1

SALMON LURES. PLATE 14

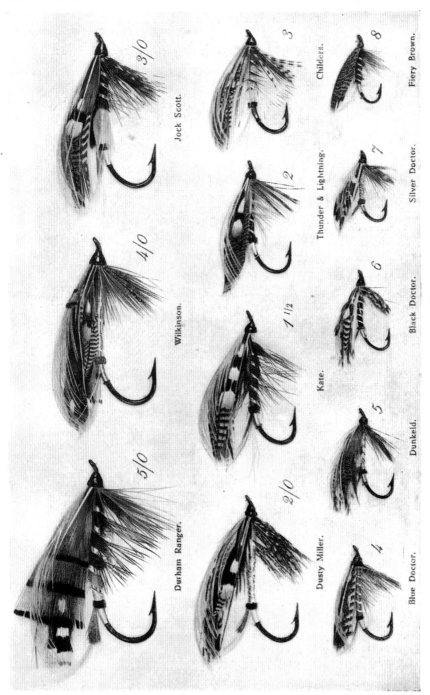

SALMON FLIES ON HARDY'S OVAL WIRE-EYED HOOKS. PLATE 15

3/0 Jock Scott.

3 Childers.

8 Fiery Brown.

2 Thunder & Lightning.

7 Silver Doctor.

4/0 Wilkinson.

7½ Kate.

6 Black Doctor.

5/0 Durham Ranger.

2/0 Dusty Miller.

5 Dunkeld.

4 Blue Doctor.

THE "MONOPLANE" SERIES. *See page* 75.

The Illustrations show the Fly as the Fish sees it except for the Jock Scott, A and B.

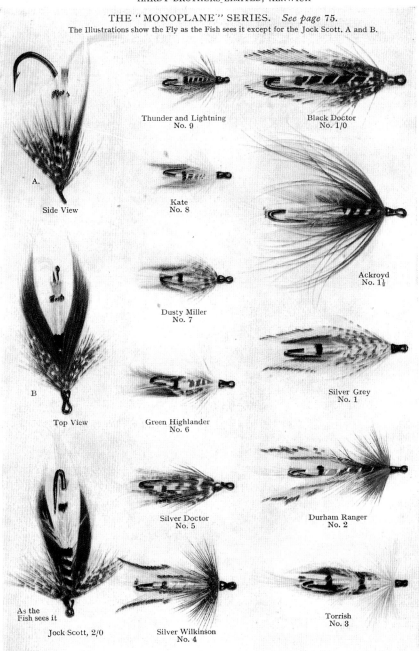

A.

Side View

Thunder and Lightning
No. 9

Kate
No. 8

Dusty Miller
No. 7

B

Top View

Green Highlander
No. 6

Silver Doctor
No. 5

As the
Fish sees it

Jock Scott, 2/0

Silver Wilkinson
No. 4

Black Doctor
No. 1/0

Ackroyd
No. 1½

Silver Grey
No. 1

Durham Ranger
No. 2

Torrish
No. 3

THE "MONOPLANE" TRANSLUFLECTING SALMON FLIES.   PLATE 16

Chapter Two

The long learning curve

'Harder should be the spirit, the heart all the bolder,
courage the greater, as the strength grows less'
Beowulf

So, with the greatest respect for all the generations of game fishers who have gone before and the many contemporary experts whose books on game fishing will always be the definitive references, we can anyway take a look at some of the more accepted opinions on salmon and sea trout, and then perhaps the more proverbial notions. Trout, being rather less complicated (because they are obliging enough to actually feed in fresh water), will be discussed later in the book. Anyone will tell you that learning about the habits of salmon and sea trout is a very long learning curve and comes through bitter experience of many years of struggling to catch fish on good, bad and indifferent water, in all conditions and at prime, middling and lousy times of the season.

Perhaps my most memorable blank week was a mid April week at Alford on the Castle Forbes water of the River Don in 1988. The river looked in perfect nick – an ideal height and crystal clear. As we eagerly assembled our rods it began lightly to snow and we were wondering whether this might be a good or bad sign, when Jimmy Ewen, the ghillie, appeared in his customary worn out old green cagoule (much stained by rolling tobacco) and wellies. *"How's it going Jimmy"* we joyfully trumpeted, *"Just fine the noo"*, replied Jimmy, *"And the fishing?"* we asked, *"Nay gid at a'"*, replied Jimmy; *"You mean no-one caught anything last week?"* we asked slightly nervously, *"Nay"* said Jimmy, *"There are nay fush"*. *"You mean there are no fish in the whole beat?"* we asked as our hearts sank, *"Aye"* said Jimmy, *"there's a couply auld kelts in th' tup pool"*. Despite this rather desperate news we availed ourselves of the opportunity of convening with nature in one of the most beautiful

Jimmy Ewen, pictured outside Castle Forbes at Alford. A life-long fisher and ghillie on the River Don, Aberdeenshire, Scotland.

parts of Scotland and, regardless of the snow, practised our casting – adhering faithfully to the all important adage, *"Ye'll nay catch a fush unless ye flee's in the watter"*.

We loved the Castle Forbes beats of the River Don so we returned for another week in the summer. We returned, also, for Jimmy's wonderful company. He wasn't your standard smartly dressed young ghillie in tweed uniform and neoprene waders, he was absolutely a part of the estate and a part of the river, he knew every lie in every pool and loved to tell us stories of his fishing days gone by. One favourite was when he was once fishing at Castle Forbes with Lady Tweedsmuir. Suddenly, she fell in up to her neck and, being utterly drenched, he was sure she would call it a day. Instead Lady Tweedsmuir stripped to *"nothin' but her braw and ponties"*, hung her clothes out to dry, and continued to fish more determined than ever!

Jimmy had an innate feel for the times when the fish might 'come on' to the take. I once asked Jimmy, now well into his seventies, whether I should be putting on a floater, a sinker or a sink tip. Jimmy looked up to the sky and after a moment's pause said, *"The croos are sirrching fir the wind"*! As a fishing proverb that was a bit too obscure for me, but the proverb exists for countrymen, and the crows will apparently take to the skies when a storm is brewing. He left me to conclude for myself what line I should put on! On the subject of fly colour Jimmy was less esoteric. I asked Jimmy what colour of fly was good for the Don, *"Red's gid"*, Jimmy replied, *"Blue…, green's awfu' gid…orange can be gid, brown… och, whitever ye feel comfortable with"*! But for me, Jimmy gave us the most important guidance when he told us that he always liked to see a hatch of flies on the water – he said that in his experience this was the best indication of when the salmon would come on to the take. He never explained why, but had seen that phenomenon on the

Aberdeenshire at her very best. The River Don at Alford on the Castle Forbes Estate, Scotland. August 1988.

river time and again. It was a wonderful August week's fishing with my father, John, and we caught four salmon and lost one.

"It's yorr locky day, sorr" announced John Thompson to my father as he prepared for another morning's salmon fishing, *"Th' day, sorr, yorr goin'ti catch a fush more stupit than you"*! John Thompson was for many years the ghillie on the Castle Grant One beat of the Spey at Grantown and he had a healthy disdain for all salmon fishers. My father once suggested that he had put together a strong team for the forthcoming week's endeavours, *"Och"* replied John, *"Give me six lucky fushers afore six experts ony day"*. Perhaps

Father and son enjoy midday refreshments beside the River Spey, Scotland. September 1990.

John's approach was a subtle ploy to make us work even harder to catch fish and prove to him that we did know a few things about salmon fishing, and it wasn't all luck!

One September week many years ago, I was lucky enough to be sharing my father's rod, along with his usual gang of fishing chums. Rain up in the hills caused the river to start to rise and John Thompson said *"you'll nay catch a fush on a rising ruver"* and called it a day. Well, this galvanised the troops. We fished on and were thankfully rewarded when Michael de Lotbiniere, always known as 'The Master Fisher' caught three good sized salmon in Congash and Slopeachor pools. Since then I have known frequent occasions when fish are caught on a rising river.

Another notion to treat with some suspicion is the one that a certain pool or a certain part of a pool is not producing fish, so is not worth fishing. Robin Upton, the 'Unguided Missile' of the fishing gang, asked John whether the far side of Congash was worth a cast or two. *"Nay"* said John, *"It doesne hold ony fush oer there"*. Of course this was red rag to a bull for Robin and he marched off alone to take the boat across the pool and give it a go. Some hours later he returned -drenched from head to foot. He had

Looking down Castle Grant One from the Garra Pool of the Spey, with high water in September 1989.

rowed across and, mooring a rope to the bank, he had eased the boat out into the stream of the pool, tied off the rope and cast out and across to cover parts of the pool that had probably not been fished in years. Third cast he was into a heavy fish and played it for a while from the boat. Not having a net (in those days we were mostly hand tailing the salmon) he decided to try and play the fish out from the bank. The current being strong he couldn't easily pull the boat into the bank by hauling on the rope, so he held the rod in his knees and started to row the boat into the side of the pool. Unfortunately one of the oars flew out of the rowlock and in trying to retrieve it, Robin joined the fish in the water. Hanging onto his rod and eventually his salmon, Robin swam to the bank and after a further struggle, landed a lovely 16 lb fish. Thankfully, he was able to retrieve the oar from the bank and returned to the fishing hut soaked through but absolutely triumphant!

I learnt from Robin that day, and ever since then I've also enjoyed trying places that are seldom fished. I reckon that, no matter what anyone says, if you think a salmon or two might be lying there, give it a go. I suppose I can relate one day in which I was quite proud of myself. Having had no luck in the morning, and believing that perhaps I was fishing a little small, I returned to the lodge to tie up a size 6 Captain Scarlet, a new pattern I had recently put together – a handsome red and orange fly with orange seal fur body, pheasant tippets to the sides, red 'ibis' wing, red hen hackle with badger hackle over and a long red 'ibis' and orange calf hair tail – magic, a work of art! I proudly showed it to John Thompson at lunch in the fishing hut and he was distinctly unimpressed! We then discussed pools for the afternoon fishing and conversation came to Craig Roy at the top of the beat, where nothing had been caught all year. It's actually a very beautiful pool and I volunteered to give it a cast.

When I arrived at Craig Roy after lunch I took the very important lead from Johnny Bridge and sat down to roll a cigarette and watch the pool. As Wellington said, *'Time spent in reconnaissance is never wasted'*, and as the old proverb goes, *'He who sits on a stone is twice glad'*! I never saw Johnny step into a pool without spending at least the time it took to puff a cigarette and take in every possible lie. Johnny taught me, therefore, to take care to read a pool

My father, John, casting a long line across the Top Sluggans, Castle Grant One on the Spey. September 1990. My father was able to wade where lighter men would be swept off their feet. In creating a boulder-like obstacle in the river, he enjoyed the thought that he was providing a resting spot for big salmon, which he would then catch!

thoroughly and plan the approach thoughtfully. By reading the pool you can see quite quickly how the fly might be presented to the salmon and whether it might be better to cast a long line from the top of the pool down and across the pool, to fish the fly slowly over a lie, or whether to cast square across the pool to fish the fly quicker.

Anyway, after a good smoke and a good read of the pool I couldn't understand why the pool was not yielding fish, as it seemed to have at least two excellent looking lies. I put on my newly tied Captain Scarlet and, to my great delight, was shortly afterwards into a nice cock salmon, which was safely tailed. After a contemplative smoke I stepped into the top of the pool again to try over the same lie. To my surprise I hooked into another cock

My father… playing one of those big salmon in the Top Sluggans on the Spey. September 1990.

Playing my sixth salmon on a red-letter day in which the party caught fourteen salmon; nine of which were on the new shrimp pattern – the 'Yabbie'. Castle Grant One, Spey, September 1990.

salmon and after a thrilling battle, safely tailed him as well. You can imagine my pride, returning to the fishing hut with two cock salmon taken from Craig Roy on my newly designed and much loved Captain Scarlet fly!

So in the seven years of salmon fishing on the famous Castle Grant beats One and Two of the Spey between 1989 and 1995 I was learning much from my father's gang of regulars and from the ghillies. Perhaps the most important lesson learnt, and well understood by all game fishers, was that rewards are brought only by perseverance.

I had a lucky day in September 1990 on Castle Grant one in which I caught six salmon on another pattern I had recently designed, the Yabbie – also a shrimp pattern, described in Stan Headley's book on 'Flies of Scotland' as *'a doddle to tie for even the least accomplished fly dresser'*! In any case it has been a successful fly on many Scottish and Irish salmon rivers and much loved by the faithful! The following day my father kindly expressed his

Not very pretty, but a 13 lb salmon is safely in the net after a lengthy battle in the relatively shallow but fast water of the Bottom Sluggans on the Spey.

delight on my success to John Thompson. John replied, *"Och, he's got some dur days comin"*!! ...and he was right! Lack of fish or poor conditions seemed to plague us all through the '93 –'95 period and fish were hard to come by.

I remember an occasion when we were all given a lesson in perseverance by 'The Master Fisher', Michael de Lotbiniere (a quite exceptional and effortless Spey caster). It had been a rather grim day with a cold south easterly autumn wind blowing straight down the river and 'into the faces of the fish'. The air temperature seemed to me colder than the water temperature and in my experience this was never a good sign for either an evening hatch of flies (remembering Jimmy Ewen's advice) or a taking

High water on the Garra Pool of the Spey at Grantown, and my efforts at Spey casting receive some 'helpful' comments from Robin Upton, Johnny Bridge and, nearest, Michael de Lotbiniere.

salmon. I returned to the fishing hut at the Garra pool to find Michael undeterred and organising the boat to row across and try a few casts into his favourite larder at the head of the pool. While the fishing party stood around clutching glasses of whisky and hooting at Michael's rowing skills,

In the ensuing 'high water Spey casting competition', Johnny Bridge shows us how it's done.

everyone agreed that the conditions were hopeless and Michael was surely wasting his time. However, as Michael got himself ready on the opposite bank, the wind dropped and a weak sun tried to filter through. Five minutes later and to our amazement we saw Michael raise his right arm as we heard the sound of a singing reel - a great sight and a great sound! A couple of seconds later, with the fish still running, Michael put his right hand to the reel and lifted into the fish. It really was a great triumph to catch a fish in those conditions and he received a hero's welcome when he returned in the boat with his salmon.

So, the salmon fishing became more circumspect for a while, but at least quiet days on the river gave one time to compose the odd ditty!

Strath Spey

As dawn reaches out her damask hand
To touch the skies with colours cool;
The ancient pine, both broad and grand
Stoops low towards the silent pool.

Deep below these peaty waters
Where current calms and eases
A salmon moves from gentle quarters
And glides to where he pleases.

And perhaps a little impatient:

Dog Days

As cattle graze in midday haze
And baking under cloudless sky;
The salmon sink to darkened depths
And watch our flies pass by.

Gladdened by our eager flogging
The fish are entertained
By oxygenating thrashing
And reputations stained.

And ready to join battle again:

The Optimist

High in spirits is the fisherman
Setting forth anew;
Working out a better plan
To catch at least a few.

Tying on a monstrous bumble
Bleary eyed and boozed;
From rock to rock he stumbled
As fish around him snoozed.

RIGHT AND FOLLOWING PAGES: Traditional lake and sea trout flies offered in the 1934 Hardy Bros. catalogue.
By kind permission of Hardy & Greys Ltd, Alnwick.

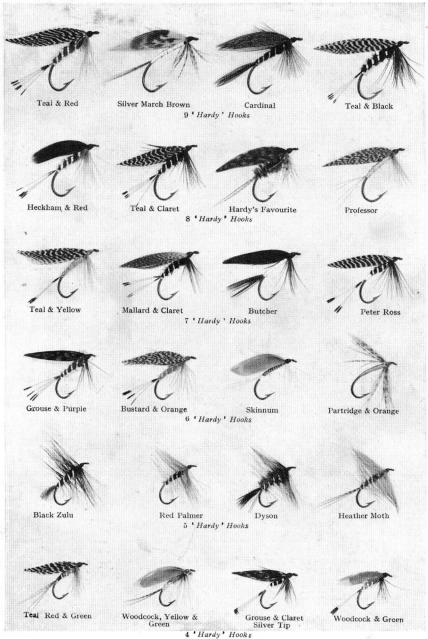

Teal & Red　　Silver March Brown　　Cardinal　　Teal & Black

9 'Hardy' Hooks

Heckham, & Red　　Teal & Claret　　Hardy's Favourite　　Professor

8 'Hardy' Hooks

Teal & Yellow　　Mallard & Claret　　Butcher　　Peter Ross

7 'Hardy' Hooks

Grouse & Purple　　Bustard & Orange　　Skinnum　　Partridge & Orange

6 'Hardy' Hooks

Black Zulu　　Red Palmer　　Dyson　　Heather Moth

5 'Hardy' Hooks

Teal Red & Green　　Woodcock, Yellow & Green　　Grouse & Claret Silver Tip　　Woodcock & Green

4 'Hardy' Hooks

LAKE AND SEA TROUT FLIES.　PLATE 9

Watson's Fancy   Mallard & Green   Woodcock & Yellow   Rogue

8 'Hardy' Hooks

Tippet & Silver   Woodcock & Red   Grouse & Claret   Alexandra

7 'Hardy' Hooks

Fiery Forbes   Major Bather   Parson Hughes   Blae & Silver

6 'Hardy' Hooks

Cinnamon   Saltoun   Blue Zulu   Teal & Green

5 'Hardy' Hooks

THE " R.C.B." FLIES

Rough Olive   Green Nymph   Corncrake Sedge   Black Nymph   Brown Nymph

4 'Hardy' Hooks

"LOCH LEVEN" FLIES

Greenwell's Glory   Butcher   Black & Blae   Dunkeld   Teal & Red

2 'Hardy' Hooks   3 'Hardy' Hooks

LAKE AND SEA TROUT FLIES. PLATE 10

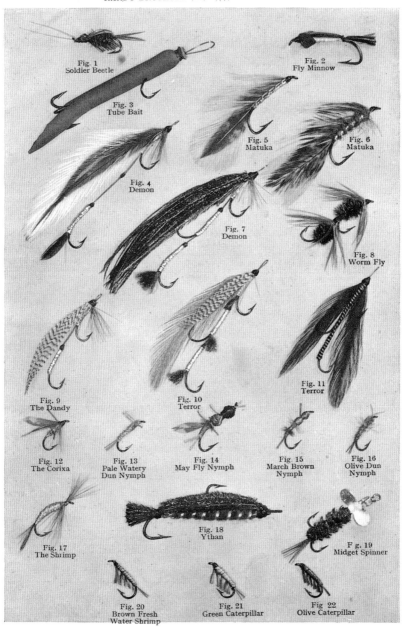

Fig. 1
Soldier Beetle

Fig. 2
Fly Minnow

Fig. 3
Tube Bait

Fig. 5
Matuka

Fig. 6
Matuka

Fig. 4
Demon

Fig. 7
Demon

Fig. 8
Worm Fly

Fig. 9
The Dandy

Fig. 10
Terror

Fig. 11
Terror

Fig. 12
The Corixa

Fig. 13
Pale Watery
Dun Nymph

Fig. 14
May Fly Nymph

Fig. 15
March Brown
Nymph

Fig. 16
Olive Dun
Nymph

Fig. 17
The Shrimp

Fig. 18
Ythan

F g. 19
Midget Spinner

Fig. 20
Brown Fresh
Water Shrimp

Fig. 21
Green Caterpillar

Fig 22
Olive Caterpillar

LURES FOR TROUT, SEA TROUT, ETC.   PLATE 11

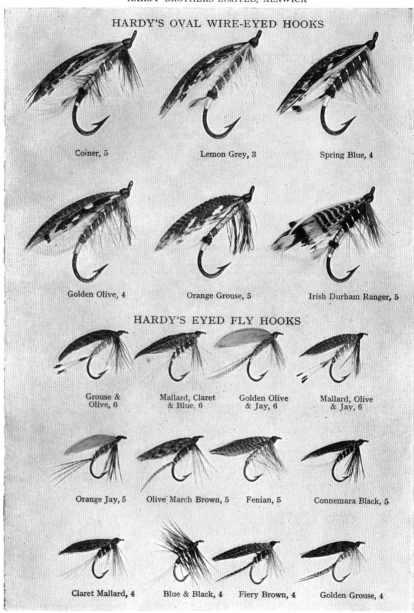

HARDY'S OVAL WIRE-EYED HOOKS

Coiner, 5   Lemon Grey, 3   Spring Blue, 4

Golden Olive, 4   Orange Grouse, 5   Irish Durham Ranger, 5

HARDY'S EYED FLY HOOKS

Grouse &   Mallard, Claret   Golden Olive   Mallard, Olive
Olive, 6   & Blue, 6   & Jay, 6   & Jay, 6

Orange Jay, 5   Olive March Brown, 5   Fenian, 5   Connemara Black, 5

Claret Mallard, 4   Blue & Black, 4   Fiery Brown, 4   Golden Grouse, 4

IRISH SALMON, LAKE AND SEA TROUT FLIES.   PLATE 17

Chapter Three

The Barometric Study

Could it be that trout and salmon physically respond to changes in barometric pressure?

'It is a capital mistake to theorise before you have data'.
Sherlock Holmes

On Saturday 9th June 1996 I was salmon fishing on the Amat Estate of the River Carron, a beautiful spate river in Ross-shire, NE Scotland. We had arrived the previous weekend, on the Sunday 4th June, to find the river in perfect condition; the river full of fresh run salmon and the river height perfect. We had a marvellous four days of fishing, catching six salmon and losing another four – a good week on any Scottish spate river (which rises and falls according to rainfall), then by Thursday the river was falling due to five days of no rain, and the conditions were becoming 'low water' – which traditionally indicate more difficult fishing conditions. On the Thursday just one fish was caught in the morning, then nothing during an afternoon of hard fishing. On Thursday night there was a sharp rainstorm, and on Friday morning the river was up again and rose during the morning. No fish were caught on the Friday, and then, on the Saturday the 9th June, although the river was by now once again in perfect condition and full of fresh run salmon – usually the most eager to come to the fly - there were no fish caught, or even attracted to the fly all day, and also not even seen jumping.

This was something I had seen, with much frustration, during the 'dur' years that John Thompson had predicted on some of the finest salmon beats in Scotland, and I wanted to know why? Why could we have caught six salmon and lost four in the first three and a half days of the week – with

Ed Troughton fishes down Bell Mackay on the Glencalvie beat of the River Carron.

salmon jumping regularly, and then in the same river and in similar water conditions (apart from the rising river on Friday morning) on the last two and a half days we not only do not catch anything, but do not see any fish either – the fish having 'gone down'? We had the latest newspaper, and through my mountaineering experience I knew about weather fronts etc and how to read a weather chart. I noted that a low front had passed through NE Scotland from the West on Thursday 7th, and that another low front was following it on Saturday 9th.

My father happened to be fishing on the River Spey in Grantown, Aberdeenshire, in the same week, and they had experienced precisely the same fishing success – fish caught in the first half of the week through to Thursday evening, then nothing on Friday and Saturday – despite conditions on the river (which has stable water levels and is not a spate river) being exactly the same on Friday and Saturday. The Grantown area is about 55 km East of Glen Carron, and would have experienced the low pressure fronts perhaps some 2-3 hours after Glen Carron depending on how fast the front was moving, but in any case their fishing experience matched ours, and I began to believe then that perhaps the fish were responding to the atmospheric or barometric pressure changes and decided, in future, to watch the barometric pressure movements whilst fishing – using the Casio Twin Sensor barometric watch I had been using for mountaineering. I began this study in July 1997. Due to the arrival of our first child in 1998 I did not fish in '98 or '99, but continued the study from 2000 to 2005.

Casting to a likely spot at the head of Vernons on the Amat beat of the River Carron.

Barometric pressure, also known as air pressure or atmospheric pressure, is the weight of air on the earth's surface. 1 litre of air has a weight of approximately 1 gram. A column of air 10 metres high and of surface area 1 cm2 (EG 1 litre of air) creates a pressure of 1g/cm2 = approximately 1 millibar. The mass of air, at 1g force (standard gravity) creates an ambient pressure of approximately 1 bar (1000 millibar) at sea level, however this changes all the time depending on the density of the air at any particular time and is affected by the movement of air over the earth's surface. The air will move from areas of higher air density (High pressure systems or anti-cyclones), which gradually weaken, into areas of low air density (Low pressure systems or cyclones), which gradually 'fill', and this movement of air is the wind. The movement is constant, and due to the spinning of the Earth, is generally from a westerly direction in the northern hemisphere and from an easterly direction in the southern hemisphere. Also due to the spinning of the Earth, the air rotates around the pressure systems and the speed of the air movement, or wind, depends on the proximity of High and Low pressure systems and the extremes of pressure between the two. On a meteorological weather chart the positions of High and Low systems are shown in circular and waving lines known as isobars, linking the areas of equal pressure. In general the wind will follow the direction of the isobars and, in the northern hemisphere, flow clockwise around High systems and anti-clockwise around Lows. If you stand with your back to the wind the centre of the Low pressure system will always be on your left. The reverse applies in the southern hemisphere.

The Park Pool, Amat, Glen Carron.

What struck me very quickly in watching the behaviour of the salmon in the river Carron was how quickly and how completely the salmon responded to even very small moves in barometric pressure. I would see a pool suddenly 'go quiet', with no fish seen jumping or moving and then seconds later sure enough the Casio watch would register a fall in barometric pressure of 1mb; or, salmon would be caught in two consecutive pools on the river at exactly the same time, and the watch would, seconds later, register a rise of just 1mb in barometric pressure. The coinciding catching of salmon by fisherman has long been observed by keen fishers and ghillies (fishing guides in Scotland), but no one has understood why – why should two different salmon grab a salmon fly at exactly the same time? The answer, I'm convinced, is because they both respond to the same rise in barometric pressure.

The behaviour of the fish during fishing trips to the river Carron from 1997 to 2005 has remained amazingly consistent – almost all of the salmon have been caught when the barometer has been stable or rising and they have generally gone quiet and refused to be interested in the fly when the barometer is falling. The very few exceptions (one fish caught on 30th July 2003 with a barometer falling 0.9 mb, two fish on the 4th May 2005 with the barometer falling 0.6 and 0.9 mb respectively, and one on the 7th May 2005 with the barometer falling 0.6 mb - out of a study total of 89 salmon) may be explained by the enthusiastic taking reputation of very fresh fish, just up from the sea and perhaps responding to a feeding reflex more influenced by feeding conditions in the sea than in the river. Fresh salmon do seem to take more readily and that is part of their great attraction. However, perhaps one can logically suppose that as the fish become more acclimatised to the fresh water, they lose their conditioned feeding instincts of the sea and adopt the conditioned feeding reflexes of fresh water –

Always a matter of personal preference, but I like to fish 'off the reel' on a low brake. If a fish takes and turns, the line can peel off for a few yards before lifting the rod and setting the hook. Tail of Bo Bahn, Amat, River Carron.

namely the conditioning of their feeding in the rivers and lakes as salmon parr and smolts. In any case the recorded catches between 1997 ('98 and '99 missed due to arrival of next generation of Bett fishers!) and 2005 show that relative to the amount of time the barometer is rising, the greatest percentage of catches are on a rising barometer (EG the best fishing conditions); then relative to the large majority of time of a stable barometer, a lower percentage of salmon caught when the barometer is steady; and very very few when the barometer is falling. The study covers 39 days and 585 hours of salmon fishing. The results of the study do appear to be absolutely conclusive, but more data is always welcome and thankfully the empirical research is being continued by one of Scotland's most experienced ghillies, Allan Donaldson of the Amat Estate on the River Carron, using a Casio barometric wristwatch and taking readings throughout the whole season.

Allan has caught over 700 salmon, his biggest 33 lbs from the Vernons pool of Amat, River Carron on the last day of the season in 2003, and his knowledge and his passion for the salmon is very well respected and appreciated by all who have had the pleasure of fishing with him. He has taught me a very great deal and not least of which is that a huge number of things must be taken into account when considering whether salmon will be likely to come onto the take or not, whether the fishing conditions are favourable or not. Water temperature and water height are crucial indicators, air temperature versus water temperature, water colour and speed (can dictate whether a pool is fishable or not), the brightness of the sun on the water and the time of the day. All these things assuming there are fish in the pools in the first place! But Allan is interested in the idea of the barometric dimension and believes that the barometric pressure may hold the answers on the days when the conditions appear perfect, but the salmon are still not taking the fly.

The thing to do then was to research whether salmon, sea trout and trout could indeed sense barometric pressure (hydrostatic pressure for underwater) changes and to what degree? Could they really detect pressure changes of as little as 1mb, or even smaller as I had observed on the river?

On the 28th May 2003 I bought an article from the Nature Web by Peter Fraser of Aberdeen University Zoology Department on fish physiology and the sensing of hydrostatic pressure in Dogfish hair cells. We had some brief e-mail correspondence, by which Peter Fraser, on 4th June 2003, wrote in response to my question *'is it possible to suggest that the swim bladder of the salmon may offer a device – via sheer and strain – to transmit or transduct*

Looking up the pools of Bridge Run, Church, Craigs, Dolly's and Sandy's in summer low water conditions on the Carron.

A heavy spring spate on the same pools. The dramatic changes to the water height in Highland spate rivers is one of their great challenges for salmon and sea trout fishers.

hydrostatic micro-pressure stimulae to the salmon?' Peter Fraser replied; *'It certainly could, although what the time course would be like and how the salmon could cope with filling or expelling air at the surface, which of course it does, we do not fully understand. The presence of the gas makes the whole system more sensitive. Yes, I think they may well respond'.* Peter Fraser recommended I contact Dr John Blaxter of Dunstaffnage Marine Research Laboratory, Oban.

John Blaxter was also very helpful with the research and sent me copies of all his relevant research on hydrostatic pressure effects on fish: **The Effects Of Pressure On Organisms 1972. Pressure Discrimination in Teleost Fish** by J. Blaxter and P Tytler, Cambridge University Press, P.433 – 436 gives proof that physostematous (open swim bladder) minnows could respond to pressures as low as 0.5 –1.0mb (0.5 – 1.0cm of H20) and that physostematous trout would respond to pressure changes as low as 1-1.5%. Also on p. 435 that *'Tsvetkov (1969), using both behavioural changes and conditioned responses in six species of freshwater fish, and submitting them to controlled rates of pressure change near atmospheric pressure, found response between 0.05 and 0.2%',* and *'There is some histological evidence of pressure receptors (proprioceptors) in the swimbladder wall and of electrophysiological activity in the swimbladder nerve (vagus) during applied pressure changes in carp, roach and rudd* (Koshtojanz & Vassilenko, 1937;Qutob ,1962).' Carp, roach and Rudd are all physostematous (open swim bladder), as is the trout, sea trout and salmon . The summary on p.439 advises that the research showed that physoclists (closed swim bladders), cod, haddock and saithe, could detect pressure changes of 0.5%.

We can note here that fish with closed swim bladders control their buoyancy in the water by secreting or absorbing gas through the wall of the swimbladder, while fish with open swim bladders control their buoyancy (as mentioned by Peter Fraser above) by filling or 'gulping' air at the surface, or also expelling air via a pneumatic or anal duct. For physostematous fish (with open swim bladder) such as the trout, sea trout and salmon, the barometric or hydrostatic (under water) pressure appears therefore to influence the depth that the fish will be positioned. Since the control of buoyancy is via surface filling of air, the higher the pressure the more we see fish on the surface, re-filling the swimbladder to maintain the desired station in the water. When the barometric pressure is low the fish have no need to keep re-filling the swim bladder and it is during these low pressure periods that the trout and salmon seem to simply disappear or 'go down'.

In **Adaptation By Cod And Saithe To Pressure Changes 1973**, reprinted from Netherlands Journal of Sea Research, J. Blaxter and P.Tytler further describe their findings on cod and saithe response to barometric pressure change – finding that *'these two species can discriminate a pressure increase of about 0.4 – 1.0% regardless of the reference pressure'*. In **Baroreception 1979** John Blaxter (from 'Sensory Ecology', Plenum Publishing Corp) indicates on p.375 the relative hydrostatic pressure to depth ratio. EG 1 atm of pressure is equal to 1000 mb which = 1033 cm H2O. Therefore 1cm of depth in water is = to 1mb of barometric (under water is hydrostatic) pressure. In observing the salmon behaviour, I had seen, as mentioned, changes in behaviour with pressure movement of as little as 1mb, and believed that even less than this was affecting fish behaviour. On p. 388 Blaxter describes spontaneous fish behaviour in a study by McCutcheon (1966) *'in the pinfish and sea bass and in nine other physoclists (with closed swim bladders) and the goldfish, a physostome (with pneumatic duct from the swimbladder to the gut). All species showed yawning behaviour if the pressure was reduced by 0.2 cm H2O (0.2 mb) for a minute or more. A cyclical swimming activity around a position in the tank to which the fish were adapted was observed when the pressure was changed by +/- 1.0 cm H2O (1mb) with the first movement being downwards for a pressure decrease and upwards for an increase'*. P. 390 offers more corroborating research – *'It is interesting that the threshold (0.001 atm equivalent to about 1 cms H2O) corresponds closely to that of the most sensitive aquatic organisms with a swimbladder'*.

As mentioned above and repeated in **Baroreception**, the Teleost fish (Any bony fish with rayed fins and a swim bladder) include the physostematous fish (fish with 'open swim bladders') and these include the salmon, sea trout and trout (salmonid) species.

On p. 392 the research reveals that *'From Table 1 Phoxinus laevis (Minnow), Lagodon rhomboids (Pinfish) and Centropristus striatus (Sea bass), it can be seen that many animals with different types of putative receptor have a threshold between 1 and 10 cms H20 (0.001 – 0.01 atm) or 0.1 – 1% above atmospheric pressure. Where gas-filled structures are present, sensitivity seems to be enhanced with a threshold of 0.1 – 1.0%'* . This was the crucial study that proved that trout, sea trout and salmon can indeed sense barometric pressure changes of as little as 1mb.

On p. 398 the research continues *'Pressure sensitivity thresholds of the order of 0.1 – 1% of adapted pressure are commonplace, especially in organisms with gas-*

Looking down the pools of Campbell's Run and Dicks on the Carron in low water. Shorter rod, small flies and a stealthy approach the order of the day.

The same pools in a tremendous spate. Suddenly the river can rise several feet in a matter of hours, after heavy rain in the hills, and sinking lines with heavy tubes are the only answer.

filled structures'. The examples given are Perch , Perca fluviatilis, with a threshold of 1.1 –1.7 cm H20 (1.1 – 1.7 mb) and Pike, Esox lucius, with a threshold of 0.5 – 0.6 cm H2O (0.5 – 0.6 mb) – so here was proof of Teleost fish able to detect barometric pressure changes as low as 0.5 mb. *'A change in atmospheric pressure of 10 mb would alter the pressure at the sea surface by 1% which would be within the sensitivity range of many fish'*.

The question of surface wave disturbance is examined on p. 399 and whether this might affect the barometric pressure as sensed by the fish. However Blaxter and Tytler in 1972 found that off the bottom, the circular movements of water below the waves tended to compensate for pressure changes.

On P. 400 under 'Gas-containing structures' the research again expects the gas containing Baroreceptors to have the greatest sensitivity since the volume changes for given pressure changes will also be the greatest, and *'The ability to appreciate changes in depth will be much enhanced near the surface; a downward movement of 1-10 cms would, for example, be appreciated at the surface, but at 90 m only downward movement of 10 – 100 cms would be sensed'*. We can therefore deduce that the sensitivity to barometric pressure change is even more enhanced in the salmon and sea trout as they enter the shallower waters of the rivers and streams.

On p. 405-406 the research concludes according to the above, and advises that the *'High sensitivities of the order of 0.1% - 1% would enable animals, especially in water, to be aware of rather small changes in depth (or hydrostatic pressure changes)...it is not at all clear why such high sensitivity seems to have been developed'*. The research was unable to explain how fish detect such small changes in barometric pressure without having these actual atmospheric pressure changes confused with the pressure changes caused by their own movements, or by the barometric 'noise' of waves and ripples on the surface of the water. However, the fact remains that this research has proven that fish detect pressure changes down to 0.5mb, and I have observed the coinciding behavioural changes of the fish in the river.

So, we can say that we do not know how the fish separate the small changes of barometric pressure from the small changes in ripple/wave height on the water – but they clearly can. If you watch salmon under water, or through the glass of a an observation tank, such as at the Tay river salmon ladder, the fish hold a perfect station in the water – regardless of the turbulence in the

The head of the Long Pool on the Carron in July with desperately low conditions. However, fish will still come to the fly on a rising barometer.

The same pool in an early summer spate. At this height very few pools are fishable, but as the river drops back and the weather front moves through, the fishing can be excellent.

water above, which must be creating hydrostatic pressure 'noise'. Blaxter and Tytler (1972), found that this 'noise' was probably compensated by circular movements of water beneath the waves. I believe therefore that the fish are able to filter out this pressure 'noise' and respond to the very small changes of actual atmospheric or barometric pressure (as little as 0.5mb) that I have observed on the river.

It has been suggested by some fishers in the past that a rising barometer increases the dissolved oxygen in the water and that this dissolved oxygen increases the metabolism of the salmon, helping to bring them onto the take. I believe the amounts of increase in oxygen in the water as the barometer rises and the decrease as the barometer falls is very small in comparison to the amount of oxygenation created by waterfalls or water turbulence. There are water falls throughout the Amat beats on the river Carron, and I have never noticed any difference in taking behaviour of salmon in the pools where there is more oxygenation from the water turbulence - which one might have expected if greater oxygenation of the water triggers a taking mood in the fish.

The Glencalvie Falls Pool, River Carron. There is plenty of oxygenation going on, but the taking moods of the salmon in this pool are no different from all the other pools on the beat.

In further work **The Effect Of Hydrostatic Pressure On Fishes,** 1980, Plenum Publishing Corp., John Blaxter on p.372 again shows important relevant research for us. I have described above how, when the barometer is falling the fish do not show on the surface of the water, but when it is rising, and when it remains high the fish are jumping regularly, and in fact, the higher the barometer the more the fish jump or splash on the surface. The fact as given on p.372 – that the Physostome (including the salmonid) has a swimbladder equipped with a duct to the exterior may well explain (as mentioned above) why salmon, sea trout and trout jump and 'rise' or splash on the surface when the barometer is rising and in particular when it is high – in order purely to 'swallow' gas to maintain buoyancy. *'Usually there is little or no gas secretion and gas is obtained by swallowing and lost by voiding. This is the 'primitive' condition present in clupeoids and salmonids and also in the Ostariophysi'.* As the barometer rises the pressure increases on the fish and it is necessary for them to maintain or add to their buoyancy by 'swallowing' air. In **Baroreception 1978** Blaxter also says of swimbladders, *'Gas will also tend to diffuse out of such structures especially at high ambient pressures'* – perhaps explaining why we particularly see the salmon on the surface when the air pressure is especially high. This would again add to the conclusion that the salmon, sea trout and trout are all highly sensitive to barometric pressure.

On P.380 Blaxter refers to the metabolic advantage of a swimbladder for maintaining buoyancy near the surface (presumably also then in rivers and lakes); and on p. 381 Blaxter again refers to the very small pressure changes to which fish will respond, *'Pressure sensors are important for fish in monitoring their vertical movements. Since the swimbladder is an adapting organ it seems unlikely that an absolute pressure sense can exist and fish are more likely to respond to pressure change'; 'Fish with swimbladders are more sensitive than those without. The swimbladder wall is probably a site for pressure-operated stretch receptors (Qutob, 1962) and it is known that swimbladder deflation in saithe leads to loss of pressure sensitivity'.* On p.382 the table 8 states that six freshwater fish were found to have pressure sensitivity down to 0.4 cms H2O (0.4 mb) – Tsvetkov (1969), and finally on P. 384 Blaxter says *'The amplitude of meteorological pressure changes is well within their sensitivity...it seems likely that fish can perceive changes in barometric pressure. Indeed the weather loach Misgurnus fossilis is said to indicate the weather by changes in its behaviour'.*

So, the research of Fraser and of Blaxter proved that the levels of sensitivity to barometric pressure changes for salmonids were at the levels I had

A good flow through Henderson's on the Glencalvie water of the River Carron, after spring rain and snow melt.

observed at the river. The next thing was to ask why salmon, sea trout and trout respond the way they do to the rising barometer? Why do the fish suddenly start being attracted to the artificial fly that the fisherman presents only, apparently, when the barometer rises – and rises by just 1mb, or even 0.5mb? The artificial fly is, of course, intended to imitate something that the fish might normally feed on. In the case of the salmon there is a difficulty because it does not actually feed when it enters the freshwater river from the sea on its return to the spawning beds of its origin, its birth. The stomach of the salmon contracts and the salmon loses weight for the 6 - 12 months that it is in the river. So why does the salmon take a fly? This has been the big question for salmon fishers for centuries – and the usual theories are that they are attacking the fly or lure out of aggression or curiosity – but not in order to feed.

I believe my research may be adding a new dimension in the understanding of the behaviour of salmon in fresh water, why they take an artificial fly and, at the same time, an understanding of the triggers that bring trout onto the feed, and why they coincide with a rise in barometric pressure.

A cock and hen salmon spawn in the late autumn head waters of the River Carron.

While watching the barometer at the river side I noticed that whenever the barometer rose, even by the 1mb micro-change that the Casio watch can display, then there would be a hatch of insects from the water – indicating that insect larvae in the water are also highly sensitive to micro changes in barometric pressure. The salmon may not feed in the river in its adult stage, but certainly in its young days after hatching, as a salmon parr and then as a smolt, for a period of 2-3 years the young salmon is feeding ferociously on aquatic beetles and insect larvae. If during this stage the salmon parr and smolts associate the rise in barometric pressure with the moment the larvae rise from the river bed (where they reside in the stones and mud) in order to hatch, then this rise in barometric pressure would trigger a Conditioned Reflex in the adult salmon when they return to the rivers to breed – causing them to snatch at any fly or lure that imitated food. The same rise in barometric pressure would also, of course, be associated by trout with the rise and hatching of insect larvae and would indicate the moment when they would come onto the fly, particularly if it imitated the type of insects that were hatching.

Sea trout will occasionally feed in fresh water but in principle it is believed the sea trout partially suppresses its appetite while returning to its breeding redds in rivers and lakes. However, sea trout appear to follow the same reaction to a rising barometric pressure and I believe they also take a fly as a conditioned reflex to the same conditions in which they fed on freshwater aquatic insects as young parr and smolts. When sea trout enter the rivers to

The Atlantic salmon parr, *Salmo salar*, with distinctive 'thumb print' markings along the lateral line. After hatching, the salmon parr remain in the freshwater rivers for two to three years before becoming a smolt.

After two to three years of feeding in freshwater as salmon parr, the young salmon become smolts, adopt the adult salmon markings and migrate downstream to the sea, usually during the spring months.

spawn, they take a fly in the same conditioned reflex feeding response as salmon. In the spring salmon fishing of May 2004, there was one occasion when I caught a salmon just as light rain began to fall (usually an indicator of a slight rise in barometric pressure) and as I landed and released the salmon my wife, Colette, noticed the swallows flying low over the river to catch the hatching insects.

Insect larvae response to hydrostatic pressure.

The next challenge was therefore to find any research that might indicate the ability of insect larvae to respond to small changes in hydrostatic pressure. I contacted the Natural History Museum Entomology Department and exchanged an e-mail with Steve Brooks on 25th June 2003. Steve Brooks advised that to date other stimuli were believed to trigger the simultaneous hatching of insect larvae – day length, temperature and angle of polarised light. However he advised that *'To my knowledge no work has been done on the influence of hydrostatic pressure and it is possible that this does act as a trigger. I suspect that the fish are responding to the presence of emerging insects'.*

I was also advised to speak to the aquatic insect expert at The Natural History Museum, Dr Peter Barnard, and he was intrigued with my suggestion and also advised that no studies had so far been done on this phenomenon. He pointed out that there are several structures on caddis fly larvae whose function is unknown, including the feathery lateral hairs along the abdomen (as distinct from the gill filaments that are prominent in some species), for example. He wondered therefore if these lateral hairs along the abdomen of the larvae were for sensing hydrostatic pressure. He asked me why I thought that insect larvae might have a need to respond to hydrostatic pressure. I said that for insects to be assured of improving weather conditions in which to hatch and breed, then they would achieve this by hatching at the moment when the barometer rises. Peter Barnard agreed this could well be an evolutionary purpose for the presence of hydrostatic pressure sensors in the insect larvae.

To check this I fished for trout on the river Test in Hampshire in May 2003, (please refer to the graph on page 160) and bought from the Met Office at Hurn the barometric readings for the 17th – 19th May 2003. The readings coincided with the insect hatching activity and the periods of trout feeding. The best fishing day was the 19th, with trout caught through the afternoon. On the 17th there was no fish feeding activity until the evening when there was a hatch of flies. The barometric readings also confirm the Met Office explanation to me for the apparent rise of barometric pressure in the summer evenings. The reason is that during a warm summer day a 'Heat Low' is created and that as the sun begins to set the land surface begins to cool and the barometer rises. This rise in pressure will be the coinciding cause of the insect larvae to rise to the surface and hatch. All trout fishers know this as the 'Evening Rise' and believed it to be triggered by angle of polarised light and water temperature changes, but that it may very well be caused by the end of the day's 'Heat Low' and the rise in pressure triggering a hatch of flies, is perhaps a new concept.

In checking lake and water temperatures I have not found that changes in temperature coincide with insect activity. In observing insect hatches throughout the day, hatches have occurred at various times on different days, and some days with no hatch at all. With polarised light being identical from one day to the next, but with very different hatching times, I also concluded that polarised light and temperature may influence the maturing time of insect larvae and pupae, but that the moment of emergence – the moment when larvae and pupae rise to the water surface to hatch is triggered by a rise in barometric pressure. This was proven without exception in my observations, and on each occasion a rise of as little as 1mb would be enough to trigger a hatch of insects. When the barometer was falling there would be no hatch.

I discussed this phenomenon with the Freshwater Biological Association on lake Windermere in Cumbria and they advised that although they had never carried out any studies on barometric pressure influence on hatching insects, they noted that some of the most prolific mayfly hatches have been seen during thunderstorms on lake Windermere. Since this was a phenomenon I had also observed – the onset of rain coinciding with a hatch of insects – I checked this with the UK Meteorological Office. They confirmed that the rain will follow just behind a low pressure front and that the moment that the rain arrives will coincide with a slight rise in barometric pressure. Rain therefore follows behind a low front and, as long as another low front is not following close behind, then the barometer will continue to rise as a high pressure system approaches. Insects will hatch during this period, despite initial rain, and can mate and lay eggs in the clear weather that follows. Trout, feeding at this time, will presumably have given rise to the well known proverb that the onset of rain is a good time to go fishing!

'He was quite pleased when he looked out and saw large drops of rain splashing in the pond'.

THE TALE OF MR JEREMY FISHER

Beatrix Potter

In **'Transduction Of Very Small Hydrostatic Pressures** – review 1998 AJ Macdonald & P.J Fraser' and using the model of a crab, Peter Fraser studied the response of aquatic animals to micro pressures via the compression of hair cells in the statocysts. On P. 26 Fraser suggests that *'a membrane with stretch-activated channels complete with cytoskeletal support is thought to account for mechano-transduction in insects'.* On p.27 Fraser refers to pressure sensitivity in decapods – the crustaceans including shrimps and prawns. Peter Barnard advised that insect larvae and crustaceans are different taxonomic Classes but are related under the same Phylum Arthropods and that it is known that separate Classes can evolve the same physiological mechanisms to respond to the same or similar natural environmental stimuli. Arthropods are any invertebrate having jointed limbs, a segmented body, and an exoskeleton made of chitin. The crab megalopae larvae, a crustacean, has been found to respond to pressure change as little as 0.028 mbar/sec *'for causing an upward swimming response'.*

One of only four salmon, in the 89 fish study, caught on a falling barometer. Allan Donaldson releases a 7½ lb fresh springer in Garvault, Carron at 16.15 on 4th May 2005.

Peter Barnard therefore indicates that although there have been no specific barometric studies on freshwater aquatic insects to date, the insect larvae in freshwater may well have developed the same hydrostatic pressure detection (hair receptors or stretch activated mechano-transducers within the exoskeleton) as the crustaceans in the sea. Fraser notes on p.27 that *'organisms lacking an obvious gas phase may still contain a small gas pocket which would provide a highly compressible phase, enabling stretch receptors to transduce micro-hydrostatic pressure changes'*. On p.29 Fraser states that *'it is now known that the thread hair receptors in the statocyst of the crab respond to small changes in hydrostatic pressure. They may therefore be the receptors which play the initial part in the animal's behavioural responses to micro-pressure. At present these sensory cells are the only micro-pressure transducers being studied'*. On p. 31 Fraser explains the mechanisms of baro-reception. The sensory element of the thread hair unit is the scolopidia and *'scolopidia are always within intero-receptors in all arthropods (which include the insects)'*, apart from Collombola which have exteroreceptive hair sensillae, and that *'In insect hair sensillae, companiform sensillae and chordotonal organs, mechanical stimulation causes a pinching or squeezing of the dendrite (which attaches to the Chorda).. In insects this sort of receptor is common'*.

Both John Blaxter and Peter Barnard advised me to contact the Director of the Freshwater Biological Association in Cumbria, regarding a possible laboratory study. The FBA advised me that the study of hydrostatic pressure influence on fresh water insect larvae was possible, but that it would take up to two years of study at a cost of £40,000/year (we hope to obtain grants for this in due course). I believe, in the meantime, that the studies so far carried out on crustaceans, a related Class in the phylum Arthropoda, as described above, gives sufficient correlating evidence that insect larvae do have the necessary baro-receptors to be responsive to pressure changes of as little as 0.5mb.

These studies convinced me that there was sufficiently compelling grounds, combined with the empirical evidence of observed insect activity on the river bank, to link the apparent feeding reflex of salmon and sea trout to a rise in barometric pressure, being due to the conditioned reflex of feeding on insect larvae as parr and smolts. All animals are creatures of habit, and if salmon are able to return not only to the river, but also to the very same pool of their birth by remembering the smell of that river and pool, perhaps as much as three or four years later, then it can logically follow that salmon would associate the appearance of food (aquatic insects) with a change in barometric pressure (a rise) – something that one can expect to be every bit as strongly imprinted on their memory as the smell of the pool and river in which they were born.

The Corner Pool, Carron, in perfect conditions. From here, in the late autumn, salmon and sea trout will run up a tiny side burn and spawn just fifty yards from this pool.

Logically, of course, the same rise in barometric pressure will trigger the same feeding response in sea trout and trout, all being related salmonids. Further evidence is offered by Blaxter again in the 1978 piece on Baroreception p. 382 *'It has become increasingly obvious in the last twenty years that many planktonic invertebrates* (which would include Arthropods) *and fish larvae without gas respond to pressure'*. On p. 383 Blaxter refers to increase in pressure causing upward movement (such as the upward movement of insect larvae from the bottom of the streams and rivers) and movement towards the light being enhanced by pressure; *'Pressure increase causes or enhances movement* (in related arthropods) *towards the light'*, and *'decreased pressure causes reduced activity or movement away from the light'* - something that Steve Brooks referred to in his e-mail from the Natural History Museum, but that we now see in studies carried out on copepods and decapods of the sea – but which are related (being crustaceans) and part of the same Arthropod Group.

Independent check on the Casio wristwatch barometric readings.

As from the Summer of 1997, apart from two missed years of fishing due to the arrival of children, I have been making all relevant barometric observations using a Twin Sensor Casio barometric watch, noting the times of fish catches and the barometric readings. It was important to double-check these readings and this was possible by obtaining the hour by hour readings of the nearest Met station.

On 29th May 2003 I bought 24 hr barometric readings from the nearest Met station to Glen Carron in Ross-shire. The readings were made at Tain, Aberdeenshire, which is 30 km East of Glen Carron and at an altitude of 4 metres above sea level. Altitude affects barometric pressure and for every 9m of height gained the barometer will drop 1mb, and will increase 1mb for every 9m descended. I wanted to be sure that the Casio barometric watch was giving accurate readings.The altitude of the Temple pool on the Amat stretch of the river Carron, where we fish, is 70 m above sea level, and therefore 66 m above the Tain Met station. The difference between the pressure reading at Tain at the same time as I read the pressure reading on my Casio watch beside the river should therefore be 66 m divided by 9m = 7.33 mb (lower than the Tain reading). On the Tain baro readings for the 7th May 2003 there is a reading at 6.00 am of 1018.2mb. I note in my fishing book for the 7th May 2003,at the same time, a reading of 1011mb – a difference of 7.2 mb.

This therefore confirmed that the Casio barometric watch was extremely accurate and ideal for the purposes of this study and for following the behaviour of the salmon and sea trout. The additional importance of the Tain Met Office readings was to show the exact trends in the barometric pressure movements, and the exact coinciding times when fish were caught. The times of the fish catches are carefully recorded by the ghillie at Amat of Glen Carron , Allan Donaldson, and all the exact records of fish catches, when and where, are in the fishing books of the Amat Estate. When at the river last spring I noted down the times of all the fish caught against the Tain readings to examine if the Tain readings agreed with my findings and also to confirm that the fish are indeed caught almost exclusively when the barometer is stable or rising.

The readings show that a steady barometer can produce fish, but a steadily rising barometer (as long as the river was not in flood) would produce the best

Unfortunately, not caught within the 39 day study in this book, but a truly magnificent salmon for Allan Donaldson at the head of the Rock Pool, Carron.

fishing; and more salmon are caught during periods of rising barometer than at any other time. On every occasion in the 39 days of the Tain barometric readings the fish are caught on a steady or rising barometer except for the fish caught, as mentioned above, on the 30th July 2003, the two fish of 4th May 2005 and the one caught on May 7th 2005 when Tain shows a slight fall in barometric pressure at the time of the catches.

The study therefore shows 89 salmon caught in 39 days, and for 85 of those salmon (96%) the Tain readings conclusively show the barometer was steady or rising, and for 4 salmon (4%) the barometer is falling. Equally important is to note how so very few salmon are caught (just 4%) in the periods when the barometer is falling. These are the 'dog days' when fishermen for years have not understood why they are not catching fish, when perhaps the day before they caught many, and yet the conditions appear the same. Many factors may account for this, but the main reason appears to be the falling barometric pressure. Certainly the evidence of the study seems to prove this, and personally I am now convinced of it.

The original empirical phenomenon, that I had observed, of the consistent behaviour of salmon to the movement of barometric pressure, and the correlating evidence for the same behaviour for sea trout and trout; the finding of research work to support it, and then the correlating barometric readings from the Met Office firmly settled the whole question according to the original theory. Salmon, sea trout and trout (the Salmonid Family) are all stimulated to feed when the barometer is rising. Thankfully salmon can

Kate's on the Carron, at an ideal height. With a box-full of favourite flies, fish in the pool, and a rising barometer – you're pretty close to heaven!

also be caught when the barometer is steady and we should be even more grateful that it appears the odd salmon will take a fly on a falling barometer (perhaps the very fresh fish), but the most prolific catch of salmon is when the barometer is steadily rising. These are the relatively rare but magical moments, when the mere act of casting a decent line with the correct size of fly will produce solid tugs and pulls almost every cast, and many more fish!

Chapter Four

The barometric breakthrough

'It can indeed raise no wonder that temerity has been generally censured; for it is one of the vices with which few can be charged, and which therefore great numbers are ready to condemn'.

Dr Johnson

This quotation probably applies even more appropriately to the salmon and sea trout fishers! It is wise not to be too bold in making observations about the behaviour of salmon and sea trout. Too many elements appear to affect their habits, and particularly their taking moods, to be definite about anything specific. However, I'm happy to admit that the evidence of my study into the effect of barometric pressure changes on salmon has utterly convinced me of its importance in explaining why salmon and sea trout have always appeared, in the past, to have unpredictable taking periods, and why I believe that with the use of a barometric instrument, such as a barometric wristwatch, we can better understand what is actually happening. The barometric pressure readings for the dates in the study can be checked at the Meteorological station in Tain, and the times of the fish caught, as mentioned before, are kept in the fishing books at Amat, Glen Carron.

Since the empirical and the laboratory studies indicated that salmonids can detect barometric pressure changes of as little as 0.5 mb, I split the categories of Rising, Stable (steady) and Falling pressure changes as follows: Rising pressure was if the barometer rose by 0.5 mb or more in the hour prior to the salmon being caught, Stable pressure was if the barometer rose or fell by no more than 0.4 mb in the hour prior to a salmon catch, and Falling pressure was if the barometer fell by 0.5 mb or more in the hour prior to the salmon catch. The study produced compelling results, and following exclusively the independent barometric readings of the Tain Met station: 85 of the 89 salmon caught in the 39 days of fishing within the study were caught on a stable or rising barometer (96%), and 4 salmon (4%) were caught on a falling barometer.

Looking down the tail of Kate's Pool into the head of Elizabeth's, and Jonny's Pot beyond, River Carron.

The fish catches are shown to the nearest hour on these coloured line charts for all the thirty nine fishing days, and the exact times of the catches and the movement of the barometer on the Tain readings are shown on the data sheets; 'R' for rising (+0.5 mb or more), 'S' for stable (+/- 0.4 mb) and 'F' for falling (-0.5 mb or less) - all corresponding to the movement of pressure in the hour previous. The days of fishing have been taken as between 7.00 am and 10.00 pm, being the possible available hours that a party might have fished on the Amat beat of the river Carron during these 39 days of the study – 15 hours per day. It is unlikely that any salmon fishing team would fish that solidly (without a break for grub and refreshments), unless sharing rods, but for the purpose of the study and to keep consistency, the fishing days were taken as 15 hours long, and the barometric pressure movements within these periods are included in the Tain barometric readings. The 39 days of 15 hours give us 585 hours of fishing. During these hours the barometric movements are not equally split between Rising, Stable and Falling. In fact the barometer is Rising for 104 hours (18% of the total 585 hours),

Stable for 420 hours (72%) and Falling for 61 hours (10%). My immediate reaction to this was that this would explain why my fishing team on the Carron had done rather well over the last 39 days of fishing!

Obviously the barometric movements can vary tremendously and you have to be very lucky to have a week with a stable or, better still, a rising barometer. Fortunately, the barometric readings during the last 39 days of our salmon fishing have given us predominantly Stable or Rising barometric pressure. Thankfully the study indicates that there is sufficient correlating insect activity on a Stable barometer to trigger a feeding response in the salmon – the conditioned reflex from their feeding activity as parr and smolts; and under these Stable barometric conditions, although the fishing is difficult, it is not impossible.

My brother, Hamish, returns a beautiful 8 lb spring salmon in Curve Pool at 12.30 2nd May 2005 on a Stable barometer.

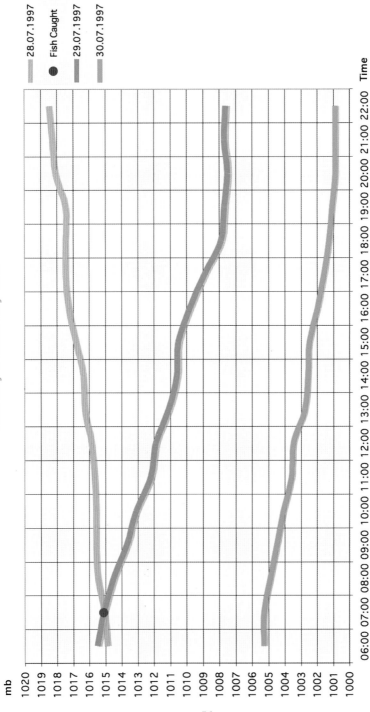

Tain Met Station barometric readings on Fishing Days and the times when Salmon were caught.
28th July to 30th July 1997

Tain Met Station

NGR = 2833E 8827N

Altitude = 4 metres

Latitude = 57:82 N Longitude = 03:97 W

Pressure at Mean Sea level (mb)

Time	28.07.1997	Movement	Salmon Caught	29.07.1997	Movement	Salmon Caught	30.07.1997	Movement	Salmon Caught
06:00	1014.9			1015.5			1005.3		
07:00	1015.1	S	07:00	1015.1	S		1005.3	S	
08:00	1015.5	S		1014.5	F		1004.9	S	
09:00	1015.6	S		1013.7	F		1004.5	S	
10:00	1015.6	S		1013.1	F		1004.1	S	
11:00	1015.7	S		1012.2	F		1003.6	F	
12:00	1015.9	S		1011.9	S		1003.5	S	
13:00	1016.3	S		1011.1	F		1002.8	F	
14:00	1016.4	S		1010.6	F		1002.6	S	
15:00	1016.9	S		1010.5	S		1002.5	S	
16:00	1017.3	R		1009.8	F		1002.0	F	
17:00	1017.5	S		1008.9	F		1001.6	S	
18:00	1017.5	S		1007.9	F		1001.3	S	
19:00	1017.5	S		1007.7	S		1001.1	S	
20:00	1018.1	R		1007.5	S		1000.9	S	
21:00	1018.3	S		1007.7	S		1000.9	S	
22:00	1018.5			1007.6			1000.9		

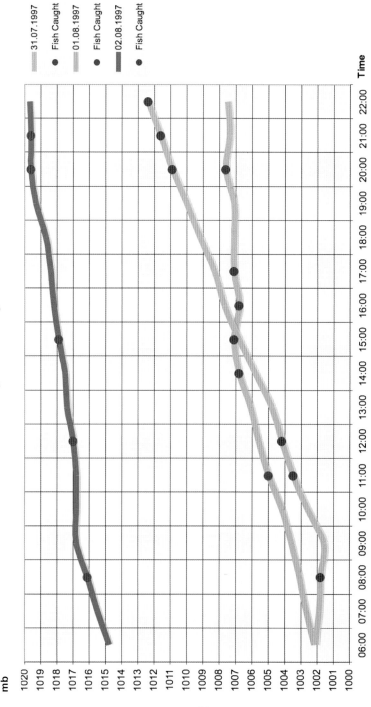

Tain Met Station barometric readings on Fishing Days and the times when Salmon were caught. 31st July to 2nd August 1997

31.07.1997
Fish Caught
01.08.1997
Fish Caught
02.08.1997
Fish Caught

Tain Met Station

NGR = 2833E 8827N

Altitude = 4 metres

Latitude = 57:82 N Longitude = 03:97 W

Pressure at Mean Sea level (mb)

Time	31.07.1997	Movement	Salmon Caught	01.08.1997	Movement	Salmon Caught	02.08.1997	Movement	Salmon Caught
06:00	1002.2			1002.1			1014.8		
07:00	1002.7	R		1001.9	S		1015.5	R	
08:00	1003.1	S		1001.8	S	08:00	1016.1	R	08:45
09:00	1003.6	R		1001.6	S		1016.8	R	
10:00	1004.2	R		1002.6	R		1016.8	S	
11:00	1005.0	R	11:15	1003.5	R	11:45	1016.8	S	
12:00	1005.6	R		1004.2	R	12:00	1017.0	S	12:00
13:00	1006.1	R		1004.8	R		1017.4	S	
14:00	1006.8	R	14:30	1005.8	R		1017.5	S	
15:00	1007.1	S	14:45	1006.8	R		1017.9	S	15:00
16:00	1006.8	S	16:30	1007.7	R		1018.2	S	
17:00	1007.1	S	17:00	1008.3	S		1018.4	S	
18:00	1007.1	S		1009.2	S		1018.7	S	
19:00	1007.1	S		1010.0	R		1019.3	R	
20:00	1007.6	R	20:40	1010.9	R	20:45	1019.6	S	20:00
21:00	1007.4	S		1011.6	R	21:00	1019.6	S	21:30
22:00	1007.5			1012.4		21:20	1019.7		

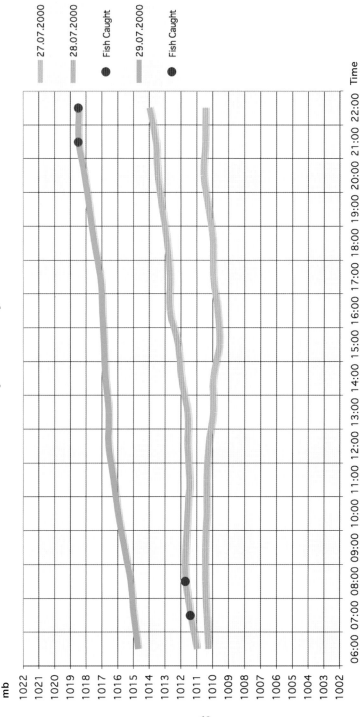

Tain Met Station barometric readings on Fishing Days and the times when Salmon were caught. 27th July to 29th July 2000

27.07.2000
28.07.2000
Fish Caught
29.07.2000
Fish Caught

mb
1022
1021
1020
1019
1018
1017
1016
1015
1014
1013
1012
1011
1010
1009
1008
1007
1006
1005
1004
1003
1002

06:00 07:00 08:00 09:00 10:00 11:00 12:00 13:00 14:00 15:00 16:00 17:00 18:00 19:00 20:00 21:00 22:00 Time

Tain Met Station

NGR = 2833E 8827N

Altitude = 4 metres

Latitude = 57:82 N Longitude = 03:97 W

Pressure at Mean Sea level (mb)

Time	27.07.2000	Movement	Salmon Caught	28.07.2000	Movement	Salmon Caught	29.07.2000	Movement	Salmon Caught
06:00	1010.3			1011.0			1014.7		
07:00	1010.4	S		1011.4	S	07:45	1015.0	S	
08:00	1010.5	S		1011.7	S	08:30	1015.2	S	
09:00	1010.5	S		1011.7	S		1015.6	S	
10:00	1010.4	S		1011.6	S		1016.0	S	
11:00	1010.4	S		1011.5	S		1016.3	S	
12:00	1010.3	S		1011.6	S		1016.6	S	
13:00	1010.0	S		1011.6	S		1016.6	S	
14:00	1010.0	S		1012.0	S		1016.8	S	
15:00	1009.6	S		1012.2	S		1016.9	S	
16:00	1009.7	S		1012.7	R		1017.0	S	
17:00	1010.0	S		1012.7	S		1017.1	S	
18:00	1010.0	S		1012.9	S		1017.5	S	
19:00	1010.3	S		1013.2	S		1017.8	S	
20:00	1010.6	S		1013.5	S		1018.1	S	
21:00	1010.5	S		1013.6	S		1018.5	S	21:40
22:00	1010.5			1014.0			1018.5	S	22:15

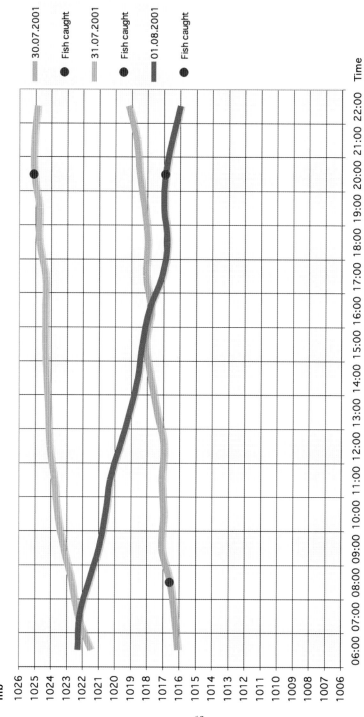

Tain Met Station barometric readings on Fishing Days and the times when Salmon were caught. 30th July to 1st August 2001

Tain Met Station

NGR = 2833E 8827N

Altitude = 4 metres

Latitude = 57:82 N Longitude = 03:97 W

Pressure at Mean Sea level (mb)

Time	30.07.2001	Movement	Salmon Caught	31.07.2001	Movement	Salmon Caught	01.08.2001	Movement	Salmon Caught
06:00	1016.1			1021.5			1022.3		
07:00	1016.3	S		1022.3	R		1022.2	S	
08:00	1016.6	S	08:10	1022.7	S		1021.6	F	
09:00	1017.1	R		1023.2	R		1021.0	F	
10:00	1017.0	S		1023.6	S		1020.6	S	
11:00	1017.1	S		1023.8	S		1020.3	S	
12:00	1017.0	S		1024.1	S		1019.7	F	
13:00	1017.4	S		1024.2	S		1019.1	F	
14:00	1017.8	S		1024.3	S		1018.6	F	
15:00	1018.1	S		1024.4	S		1018.3	S	
16:00	1017.8	S		1024.4	S		1017.9	S	
17:00	1018.1	S		1024.4	S		1017.1	F	
18:00	1018.0	S		1024.8	S		1016.8	S	
19:00	1018.2	S		1024.8	S		1017.0	S	
20:00	1018.5	S		1025.1	S	20:30	1016.9	S	20:00
21:00	1018.7	S		1025.1	S		1016.5	S	
22:00	1019.2			1024.9			1016.0		

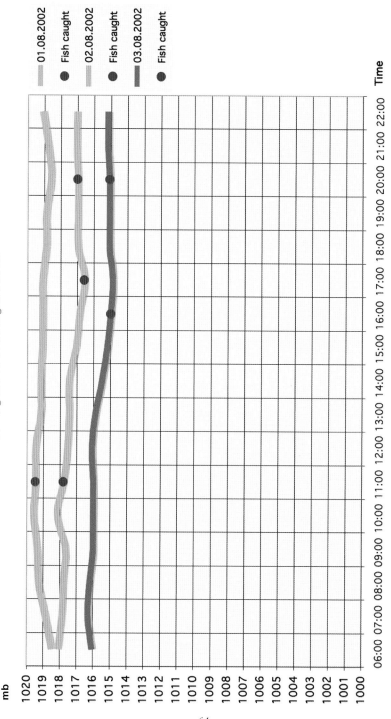

Tain Met Station barometric readings on Fishing Days and the times when Salmon were caught. 1st August to 3rd August 2002

01.08.2002
Fish caught
02.08.2002
Fish caught
03.08.2002
Fish caught

Tain Met Station

NGR = 2833E 8827N

Altitude = 4 metres

Latitude = 57:82 N Longitude = 03:97 W

Pressure at Mean Sea level (mb)

Time	01.08.2002	Movement	Salmon Caught	02.08.2002	Movement	Salmon Caught	03.08.2002	Movement	Salmon Caught
06:00	1018.5			1018.1			1016.1		
07:00	1018.9	S		1017.9	S		1016.3	S	
08:00	1019.3	S		1017.8	S		1016.2	S	
09:00	1019.4	S		1017.7	S		1016.0	S	
10:00	1019.6	S		1018.2	S		1016.0	S	
11:00	1019.5	S	11:55	1017.8	S	11:00	1016.0	S	
12:00	1019.5	S		1017.6	S		1016.1	S	
13:00	1019.2	S		1017.5	S		1015.9	S	
14:00	1019.2	S		1017.5	S		1015.5	S	
15:00	1019.1	S		1017.1	S		1015.2	S	
16:00	1019.1	S		1016.9	S		1015.0	S	16:15
17:00	1019.1	S		1016.6	S	17:00	1014.9	S	
18:00	1018.9	S		1017.0	S		1015.1	S	
19:00	1018.9	S		1017.0	S		1015.1	S	
20:00	1018.6	S		1017.0	S	20:15	1015.1	S	20:00
21:00	1018.8	S		1017.1	S		1015.2	S	
22:00	1019.1			1017.1			1015.2		

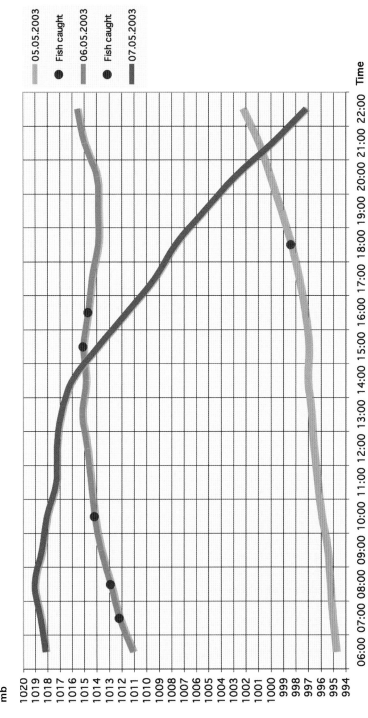

Tain Met Station barometric readings on Fishing Days and the times when Salmon were caught. 5th May to 7th May 2003

05.05.2003
Fish caught
06.05.2003
Fish caught
07.05.2003

Tain Met Station
NGR = 2833E 8827N
Altitude = 4 metres
Latitude = 57:82 N Longitude = 03:97 W
Pressure at Mean Sea level (mb)

Time	05.05.2003	Movement	Salmon Caught	06.05.2003	Movement	Salmon Caught	07.05.2003	Movement	Salmon Caught
06:00	994.8			1011.1			1018.2		
07:00	995.1	S		1012.2	R	07:25	1018.6	S	
08:00	995.3	S		1012.9	R	07:30	1019.1	R	
09:00	995.5	S		1013.7	R		1018.5	F	
10:00	996.0	R		1014.2	R	10:00	1018.1	S	
11:00	996.3	S		1014.5	S		1017.3	S	
12:00	996.6	S		1014.8	S		1017.3	S	
13:00	996.8	S		1015.2	S		1016.9	S	
14:00	997.1	S		1014.9	S		1016.0	F	
15:00	997.0	S		1015.1	S	15:15	1013.9	F	
16:00	997.3	S		1014.7	S	15:50	1011.6	F	
17:00	997.8	R		1014.4	S		1009.4	F	
18:00	998.4	R	18:45	1013.9	F		1007.7	F	
19:00	999.2	R		1013.9	S		1005.4	F	
20:00	1000.1	R		1014.0	S		1002.9	F	
21:00	1001.0	R		1015.0	R		999.9	F	
22:00	1002.3			1015.6			997.2		

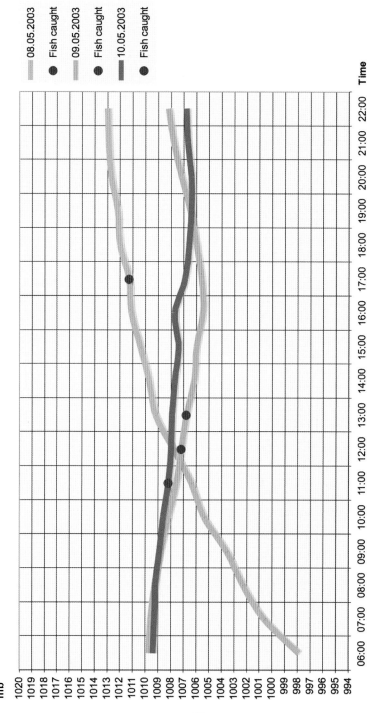

Tain Met Station barometric readings on Fishing Days and the times when Salmon were caught.
8th May to 10th May 2003

Tain Met Station
NGR = 2833E 8827N
Altitude = 4 metres
Latitude = 57:82 N Longitude = 03:97 W
Pressure at Mean Sea level (mb)

Time	08.05.2003	Movement	Salmon Caught	09.05.2003	Movement	Salmon Caught	10.05.2003	Movement	Salmon Caught
06:00	997.9			1009.7			1009.4		
07:00	1000.6	R		1009.6	S		1009.3	S	
08:00	1002.3	R		1009.3	S		1009.2	S	
09:00	1003.6	R		1008.8	F		1008.9	S	
10:00	1005.4	R		1008.2	F		1008.6	S	
11:00	1006.4	R		1007.6	F		1008.2	S	11:00
12:00	1007.8	R		1007.2	S	12:00	1008.0	S	
13:00	1009.2	R		1006.8	S	12:10	1007.9	S	
14:00	1009.7	R		1006.2	F		1007.7	S	
15:00	1010.4	R		1006.0	S		1007.4	S	
16:00	1011.1	R		1005.5	F		1007.7	S	
17:00	1011.3	S	17:00	1005.6	S		1006.9	F	
18:00	1012.0	R		1006.0	S		1006.6	S	
19:00	1012.2	S		1006.5	R		1006.4	S	
20:00	1012.7	R		1007.2	R		1006.4	S	
21:00	1012.9	S		1007.8	R		1006.7	S	
22:00	1013.0			1008.2			1006.8		

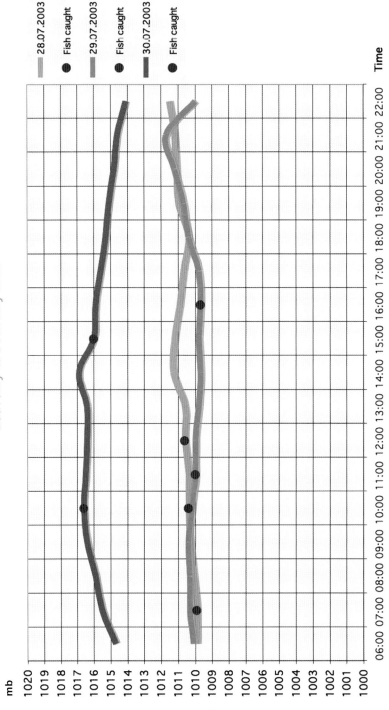

Tain Met Station barometric readings on Fishing Days and the times when Salmon were caught. 28th July to 30th July 2003

mb

1020 1019 1018 1017 1016 1015 1014 1013 1012 1011 1010 1009 1008 1007 1006 1005 1004 1003 1002 1001 1000

06:00 07:00 08:00 09:00 10:00 11:00 12:00 13:00 14:00 15:00 16:00 17:00 18:00 19:00 20:00 21:00 22:00

Time

28.07.2003
● Fish caught
29.07.2003
● Fish caught
30.07.2003
● Fish caught

Tain Met Station

NGR = 2833E 8827N

Altitude = 4 metres

Latitude = 57:82 N Longitude = 03:97 W

Pressure at Mean Sea level (mb)

Time	28.07.2003	Movement	Salmon Caught	29.07.2003	Movement	Salmon Caught	30.07.2003	Movement	Salmon Caught
06:00	1009.9			1010.1			1014.7		
07:00	1009.9	S	7.35	1010.3	S		1015.5	S	
08:00	1010.1	S		1010.3	S		1015.9	S	
09:00	1010.3	S		1010.4	S		1016.4	R	
10:00	1010.4	S	10.30	1010.2	S		1016.6	S	10.30
11:00	1010.4	S		1010.0	S	11.15	1016.5	S	
12:00	1010.6	S	12.15	1010.0	S		1016.4	S	
13:00	1010.6	S		1009.8	S		1016.4	S	
14:00	1011.3	R		1009.7	S		1016.9	R	
15:00	1011.2	S		1009.8	S		1016.0	F	15.30
16:00	1010.9	S		1009.7	S	16.30	1015.9	S	
17:00	1010.7	S		1009.8	S		1015.6	S	
18:00	1010.4	S		1010.4	R		1015.3	S	
19:00	1011.0	R		1010.7	S		1015.1	S	
20:00	1011.1	S		1011.2	R		1014.8	S	
21:00	1011.2	S		1011.7	R		1014.6	S	
22:00	1011.5			1012.0			1014.1		

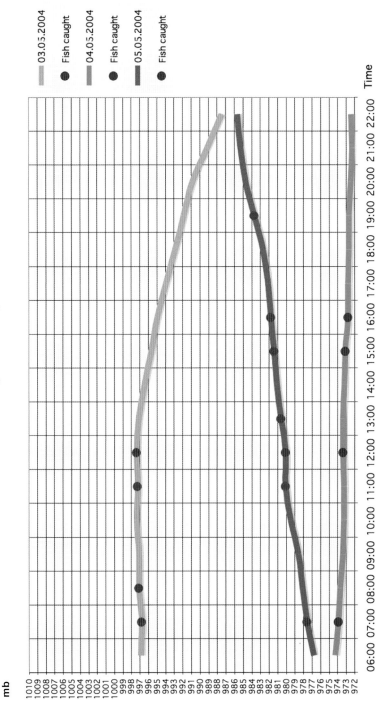

Tain Met Station barometric readings on Fishing Days and the times when Salmon were caught. 3rd May to 5th May 2004

Tain Met Station

NGR = 2833E 8827N

Altitude = 4 metres

Latitude = 57:82 N Longitude = 03:97 W

Pressure at Mean Sea level (mb)

Time	03.05.2004	Movement	Caught	04.05.2004	Movement	Caught	05.05.2004	Movement	Caught
06:00	996.9			974.3			976.8		
07:00	996.8	S	7.25	973.9	S	7.40	977.6	R	7.30
08:00	997.1	S	7.25	973.7	S		978.1	R	
09:00	997.1	S		973.4	S		978.6	R	
10:00	997.4	S		973.3	S		979.5	R	
11:00	997.3	S	11.35	973.3	S		980.1	R	11.45
12:00	997.4	S	12.30	973.4	S	12.40	980.1	S	12.00
13:00	997.2	S		973.4	S		980.6	R	12.15
14:00	996.5	F		973.2	S		981.1	R	
15:00	995.7	F		973.1	S	15.30	981.4	S	15.30
16:00	995.0	F		972.8	S	15.30	981.8	S	15.45
17:00	994.0	F		972.8	S		982.1	S	
18:00	992.9	F		972.7	S		982.7	R	
19:00	991.9	F		972.7	S		983.7	R	19.00
20:00	990.9	F		972.5	S		984.7	R	
21:00	989.2	F		972.3	S		985.3	R	
22:00	987.5			972.4			985.7		

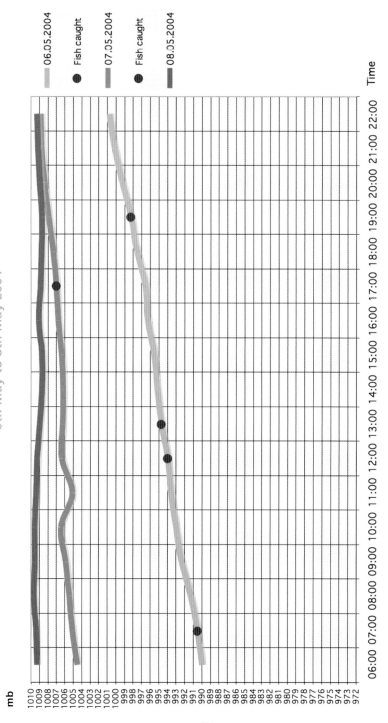

Tain Met Station barometric readings on Fishing Days and the times when Salmon were caught.
6th May to 8th May 2004

06.05.2004
Fish caught
07.05.2004
Fish caught
08.05.2004

mb

1010
1009
1008
1007
1006
1005
1004
1003
1002
1001
1000
999
998
997
996
995
994
993
992
991
990
989
988
987
986
985
984
983
982
981
980
979
978
977
976
975
974
973
972

06:00 07:00 08:00 09:00 10:00 11:00 12:00 13:00 14:00 15:00 16:00 17:00 18:00 19:00 20:00 21:00 22:00

Time

Tain Met Station

NGR = 2833E 8827N

Altitude = 4 metres

Latitude = 57·82 N Longitude = 03·97 W

Pressure at Mean Sea level (mb)

Time	06.05.2004	Movement	Salmon Caught	07.05.2004	Movement	Salmon Caught	08.05.2004	Movement	Salmon Caught
06:00	990.0			1004.5			1009.3		
07:00	990.5	R	7.04	1005.1	R		1009.4	S	
08:00	991.3	R		1005.5	S		1009.7	S	
09:00	992.4	R		1005.9	S		1009.6	S	
10:00	993.0	R		1006.2	S		1009.6	S	
11:00	993.6	R		1006.1	S		1009.4	S	
12:00	994.0	S	12.20	1006.4	S		1009.3	S	
13:00	994.7	R	12.45	1006.3	S		1009.0	S	
14:00	995.2	R		1006.2	S		1008.7	S	
15:00	995.6	S		1006.4	S		1008.7	S	
16:00	996.3	R		1006.7	S		1009.1	S	
17:00	996.6	S		1007.0	S	17.00	1008.9	S	
18:00	997.6	R		1007.4	S		1008.8	S	
19:00	998.3	R	19.50	1007.9	R		1008.7	S	
20:00	999.3	R		1008.4	R		1009.0	S	
21:00	1000.2	R		1008.8	S		1009.2	S	
22:00	1000.8			1008.9			1009.3		

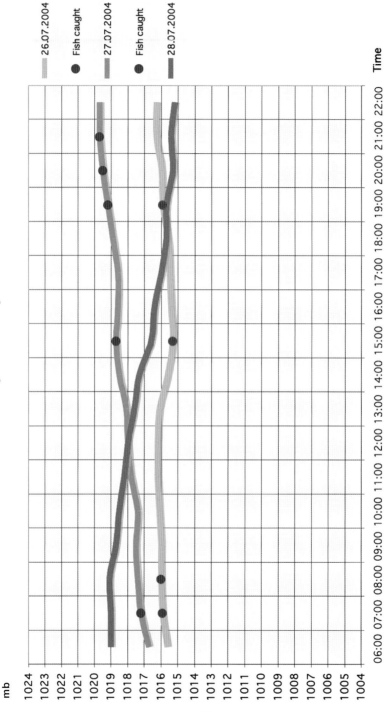

Tain Met Station barometric readings on Fishing Days and the times when Salmon were caught. 26th July to 29th July 2004

26.07.2004
Fish caught
27.07.2004
Fish caught
28.07.2004

mb

1024 1023 1022 1021 1020 1019 1018 1017 1016 1015 1014 1013 1012 1011 1010 1009 1008 1007 1006 1005 1004

06:00 07:00 08:00 09:00 10:00 11:00 12:00 13:00 14:00 15:00 16:00 17:00 18:00 19:00 20:00 21:00 22:00

Time

Tain Met Station

NGR = 2833E 8827N

Altitude = 4 metres

Latitude = 57:82 N Longitude = 03:97 W

Pressure at Mean Sea level (mb)

Time	26.07.2004	Movement	Salmon Caught	27.07.2004	Movement	Salmon Caught	28.07.2004	Movement	Salmon Caught
06:00	1015.6			1016.7			1019.0		
07:00	1015.9	S	7.40	1017.2	R	7.30	1019.0	S	
08:00	1016.0	S	8.15	1017.4	S		1019.1	S	
09:00	1016.0	S		1017.5	S		1018.7	F	
10:00	1016.1	S		1017.4	S		1018.5	S	
11:00	1016.2	S		1017.8	S		1018.2	S	
12:00	1016.2	S		1018.0	S		1018.0	S	
13:00	1016.1	S		1018.1	S		1017.6	S	
14:00	1015.6	F		1018.5	S		1017.3	S	
15:00	1015.3	S	15.15	1018.7	S	15.15	1016.6	F	
16:00	1015.4	S		1018.6	S		1016.4	S	
17:00	1015.5	S		1018.6	S		1016.0	S	
18:00	1015.6	S		1018.9	S		1015.7	S	
19:00	1015.9	S	19.00	1019.2	S	19.20	1015.7	S	
20:00	1016.0			1019.5	S	20.50	1015.3	S	
21:00	1016.3	S		1019.7	S	21.30	1015.4	S	
22:00	1016.3			1019.7			1015.2		

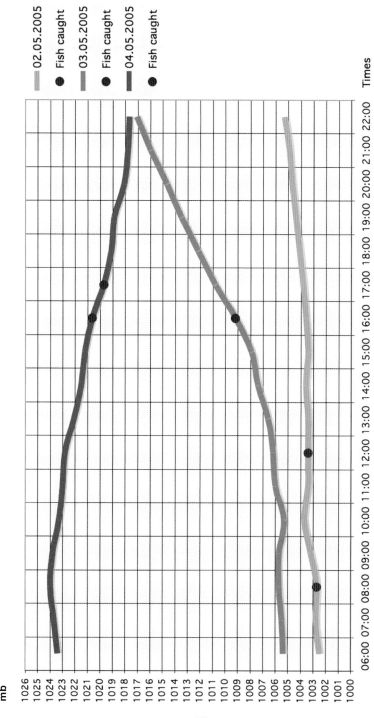

Tain Met Station barometric readings on Fishing Days and the times when Salmon were caught. 2nd May to 4th May 2005

Tain Met Station

NGR = 2833E 8827N

Altitude = 4 metres

Latitude = 57:82 N Longitude = 03:97 W

Pressure at Mean Sea level (mb)

Time	02.05.2005	Movement	Salmon Caught	03.05.2005	Movement	Salmon Caught	04.05.2005	Movement	Salmon Caught
06:00	1002.5			1005.4			1023.4		
07:00	1002.8	S		1005.5	S		1023.7	S	
08:00	1002.7	S	08:50	1005.7	S		1024.0	S	
09:00	1003.2	R		1005.7	S		1023.8	S	
10:00	1003.7	R		1005.3	S		1023.3	F	
11:00	1003.4	S		1006.0	R	11:30	1023.0	S	
12:00	1003.4	S	12:30	1006.2	S		1022.8	S	
13:00	1003.4	S		1006.6	S		1022.1	F	
14:00	1003.6	S		1007.4	R		1021.5	F	
15:00	1003.4	S		1007.9	R		1021.2	S	
16:00	1003.6	S		1009.2	R		1020.6	F	16:15
17:00	1003.8	S		1010.8	R		1019.7	F	16:45
18:00	1004.1	S		1012.2	R		1019.1	F	
19:00	1004.4	S		1013.5	R		1018.9	S	
20:00	1004.7	S		1014.7	R		1018.1	F	
21:00	1004.9	S		1016.0	R		1017.8	S	
22:00	1005.3			1017.1			1017.7		

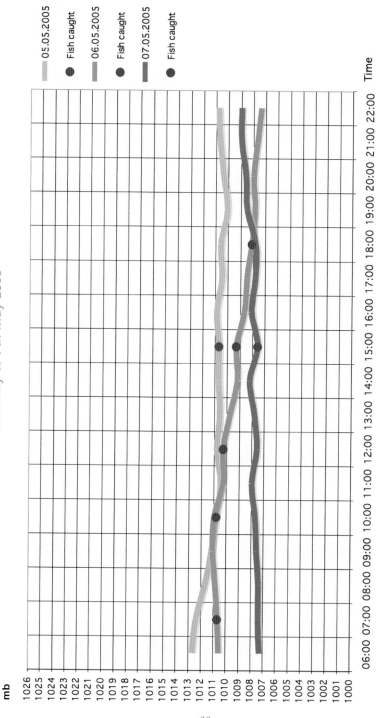

Tain Met Station barometric readings on Fishing Days and the times when Salmon were caught.
5th May to 7th May 2005

05.05.2005
Fish caught
06.05.2005
Fish caught
07.05.2005
Fish caught

mb

1026
1025
1024
1023
1022
1021
1020
1019
1018
1017
1016
1015
1014
1013
1012
1011
1010
1009
1008
1007
1006
1005
1004
1003
1002
1001
1000

06:00 07:00 08:00 09:00 10:00 11:00 12:00 13:00 14:00 15:00 16:00 17:00 18:00 19:00 20:00 21:00 22:00

Time

Tain Met Station

NGR = 2833E 8827N

Altitude = 4 metres

Latitude = 57:82 N Longitude = 03:97 W

Pressure at Mean Sea level (mb)

Time	05.05.2005	Movement	Salmon Caught	06.05.2005	Movement	Salmon Caught	07.05.2005	Movement	Salmon Caught
06:00	1012.7			1010.6			1007.3		
07:00	1012.4	S		1010.7	S	07:45	1007.4	S	
08:00	1011.7	F		1010.9	S		1007.4	S	
09:00	1011.2	F		1011.1	S		1007.6	S	
10:00	1010.8	S	10:30	1011.0	S		1007.7	S	
11:00	1010.5	S		1010.3	F		1008.0	S	
12:00	1010.8	S		1010.3	S	12:15	1007.6	S	
13:00	1010.6	S		1009.8	F		1007.8	S	
14:00	1010.7	S		1009.2	F		1008.2	S	
15:00	1010.7	S	15:40	1009.3	S	15:45	1007.6	F	15:35
16:00	1010.9	S		1008.7	F		1008.1	R	
17:00	1010.5	S		1008.5	S		1007.8	S	
18:00	1010.6	S		1008.1	S	18:20	1007.8	S	
19:00	1010.1	F		1007.9	S		1008.5	R	
20:00	1010.4	S		1008.0	S		1008.6	S	
21:00	1010.7	S		1007.7	S		1009.0	S	
22:00	1010.8			1007.4			1009.0		

Allan Donaldson is taken by a strong fish in Park Pool. Amat Lodge, and also Allan and Jean's new house overlook this spectacular pool on the Carron.

Of the 89 salmon caught in the study, 64 (72%) are caught on the Stable barometer. If barometric pressure was of no significance to the feeding habits of salmonids then we might have expected the salmon catches to have been equally reflected in the Rising and Falling barometric periods, EG 18% for the Rising period and 10% for the Falling period. However, as mentioned above, this is not the case. Only 4% (4 salmon) of the salmon are caught when the barometer is Falling, despite this being 10% (61 hours) of the 585 hours of fishing, and 24% (21 salmon) are caught during the Rising period, despite it being only 18% of the 585 hours. This, I believe, is truly the barometric breakthrough that has been wondered about for years but only really confirmed now, in this study.

So, 21 salmon are caught in 104 hours of Rising barometer, 64 salmon are caught in 420 hours of Stable barometer, and 4 salmon are caught in 61 hours of Falling barometer. These results mean that on a Rising barometer, based on the full 15 hour fishing day of this study, we caught a salmon every 5 hours; on a Stable barometer we caught a salmon every 6.6 hours, and on a Falling barometer we caught a salmon every 15.3 hours. The huge difference in strike rate between Stable or more particularly Rising barometric conditions and that of Falling barometric pressure tells a story of its own, and no doubt we all have grim memories of flogging for hour after hour, sometimes in apparently good conditions, even sometimes over fish we can actually see – all to no avail.

Allan nets a salmon for my wife, Colette, in Park Pool.

Colette with her magnificent 10 lb spring salmon prior to release, caught at 15.45 6th May 2005 on a Stable barometer.

As mentioned above, these must be the 'Dog Days' when we try every fly in the box and spend hours 'brute bothering', casting repeatedly over the known lies. Thankfully, although these days will still come and go, they can be greeted philosophically. We can now glance at our barometric watch and console ourselves that the barometric conditions are not with us and we must either try harder, and be prepared for disappointment, or go home for an early beer. These results are certainly ringing bells with me on the sort of fishing conditions and success rates in the twenty-seven years I have been chasing salmon; although, until recently, I feel I may have been plagued by the falling barometer rather more than my fair share! But I would accept that for about 70% of the time the fishing has been difficult, but not impossible – akin perhaps to a Stable barometer and then one can expect another 15% of the time to be almost impossible on a Falling barometer and 15% absolutely brilliant with the barometer Rising – depending entirely on how lucky you are with the barometric movements during your allotted days beside the river.

In the results of this 39 day study and, as I say, strictly following 15 hours of fishing on every day (regardless of spring or summer), the findings show that you are almost 1½ times more likely to catch a salmon on a Rising barometer than on a Stable barometer, and 3 times more likely to catch a salmon on a Rising barometer than on a Falling barometer. There's no doubt about it – when you go salmon fishing you most definitely want to see the barometer rising on your barometric wristwatch! The study, therefore, shows three times as many salmon caught when the barometer is rising than when it is falling. For fishers who enjoy a tough challenge, and this must surely include all salmon fishers, then to catch a salmon on a falling barometer has to be the toughest challenge of all!

The days used in the study are all the days I was personally fishing on the Amat Estate of the river Carron and no days were excluded from the study, thereby ensuring a true representation, with fishing conditions varying from huge water in the spring with fresh run spring salmon, to very low water conditions in July with fresh grilse and long resident spring fish. Water temperatures were taken regularly and these would fluctuate quite dramatically, as is well known already, but the fluctuation did not appear to affect or influence the taking mood of the fish in isolation, but remain an important factor – to my mind principally in determining the fly size.

Studies made into the possible correlation of salmon taking times and water temperature changes have added to the debate, as have been the studies

Allan Donaldson and Colette, after her salmon has been safely returned.

into the influence of dissolved oxygen. However, the deciding factor for me is the well known phenomenon of salmon suddenly coming onto the take in pools up and down the beat at exactly the same time, and going off the take equally suddenly at the same time. Water temperature and dissolved oxygen content does not change anything like as dramatically as these short taking periods. Another factor acts as the final trigger, and the study has certainly persuaded me that it can only be barometric pressure. In the 39 days of the study an amazingly high proportion of the salmon (41 fish, 46%) are caught within 45 minutes of each other, either by the same fisher in the same pool, or by different fishers in different pools on the beat, and all corresponding with a rise in the barometric pressure. In the spring we fish no less than eight hours per day and in the summer perhaps even ten hours, if the conditions are not too bright. To find that almost half the fish are caught within no more than 45 minutes of each other, many within just 15 minutes of each other, indicates how long we fish without catching salmon, and how rarely they do actually come onto the take. Hence the

A raging torrent through Park Pool after very heavy rain-storms make the river almost unrecognisable.

sheer thrill when the knock on the rod finally comes, and the line peels off the reel; the heart is pounding and the mixture of surprise and delight almost overwhelming!

Therefore, with salmon coming onto the take relatively rarely, it pays to be as ready for the moment as you can. I'm not saying that a barometric watch will tell you the precise moment when a salmon will take, but it certainly gives you a strong lead. I would never go out trout or salmon fishing without my barometric watch. It is now the sixth sense that I rely on to indicate what is happening with the fish and, on one pre breakfast session two years ago, when I forgot the watch, I felt utterly bereft! I suppose there must be a few barometric watches available on the market, principally for sailing and mountaineering, but the one I have used for the study is the Casio Twin Sensor, recently up-graded to a Triple Sensor (to include a compass facility), and it is perfect for the sport and game fisher. It's accuracy has been proven by the double checking with two different Met offices in Tain and

The Casio Triple Sensor barometric watch. The barometric display shows a sharply rising pressure of 7 mb over a 12 hour period within the previous 26 hours – an excellent 12 hour period for trout and salmon fishing.

Hurn, and it has the facility of a graph, showing the barometric pressure readings over the last 26 hours, taken at two hour intervals. Most importantly the watch can be up-dated at any time to give the current barometric pressure, and this is done by the quick press of a button.

My fishing friends are all now using the Casio Triple Sensor barometric watch and are already as dedicated to it, as a fishing tool, as I am. The beauty of a watch as opposed to some sort of other pocket device is that while you are actually fishing, with the rod in one hand, you can quickly see what the barometric pressure is doing by just lifting a finger off the rod

Park Pool at sunset, and with the height coming back into an excellent spring condition after the heavy spate.

handle and pressing the 'baro' button on the right hand side of the watch. I check the barometer every ten to twenty minutes so to be able do it quickly, without stopping fishing, is important. If you see a hatch of flies, check the barometer and see if it is either stable or rising. Other times one sees the barometer rise and shortly afterwards a hatch will follow.

The Casio Triple Sensor watch is sensitive down to 1mb pressure, but the scientific studies indicate that physostematous fish, which include the salmonids, can detect pressure change down to 0.5mb, and that Arthropods, which include aquatic insects, can also detect pressure change down to 0.5mb. Therefore, a stable barometer as shown on the Casio, is still an indicator of reasonable fishing conditions, since the pressure can move up by 0.5 mb and bring the fish onto the take, but still show as stable on the watch. But, as the study has shown, so long as there are fish in the pools, what we are really wanting is a steadily rising barometer. Therefore, when the watch shows a rise of 1mb things are definitely looking up, and we need to concentrate all the more on the casting and be extra ready for the take. As mentioned before, the falling barometer is bad news, but at least when you see the barometer falling on the watch, you understand why you are not catching fish and can relax a little. You can genuinely say to yourself that it's the falling pressure that's at fault – not your fishing!

Why do salmon 'take short'?

The barometric study shows us a sliding scale of salmon behaviour. The steadily rising barometer appeared to bring the salmon on more strongly, then the steady barometer also produced fish, but less easily, and then the falling barometer produced four fish but only on three days out of the thirty-nine. Salmon fishers have all experienced the different taking ways of the fish, and this has been another fascinating subject and talking point for years. We have all experienced the frustrating periods when salmon 'take short'; and when salmon are lightly hooked and lost in much higher proportions. At these times the salmon are very often hooked in the kype or in the front of the mouth. Also at these times, the salmon take 'on the dangle' at the end of the cast; they are on for a second or two, then lost. This is all the harder to bear, because the 'short taking' periods seem to coincide with difficult fishing conditions, when the salmon are harder to come by and, when they do take, they are on and off in a beat of the heart.

In the seven years of watching my barometer while salmon fishing I have

George Andrews works his way down Temple Pool to the main taking spot, at this height of water, under the copper beech.

noticed that the frustrating periods of 'short taking' salmon have coincided with the periods when the barometer has been steady. These are the periods when there is almost no change in the weather and on the weather chart you find yourself in the middle of a huge slow moving anti-cyclone - a weak High pressure system with occasional slow moving cold fronts. In any case, from experience, the stable barometer seems to explain the behaviour of the salmon. They will take a fly, but less eagerly. The study shows that the odd salmon can be picked up even when the barometer is falling, but in my experience, even less enthusiastically! On the few occasions when this has happened - on the four occasions in the study, including the two days in spring this year (2005) - the fish were very fresh into the river and, as mentioned earlier, may still be responding to feeding reflexes redolent of their feeding in the sea (with no apparent barometric pressure relevance, at least that has been so far studied), rather than a feeding reflex that is conditioned by their feeding as parr and smolts in the river. In other words, the longer the salmon stay in the river, the fresh water, the more they become conditioned to the feeding responses of their time as parr and smolts and respond more readily to a rising barometer, and the more steadily it rises the more readily they respond.

Annabelle Remnant returns an absolute 'bar of silver' to the tail of Temple Pool. She caught this magnificent 10 lb salmon at 10.30 am 5th May 2005 on a Stable barometer.

The suppression of feeding by salmon when they enter fresh water is logically explained by the need to protect the populations of young salmon parr and smolts that were spawned in the river between one and three years previously. Returning salmon in huge numbers would also have depleted the natural food source in the rivers, needed by the maturing parr and smolts. Before commercial netting at sea, decimation of sea feeding grounds and river pollution, the rivers of Britain and Ireland were possibly as prolific with returning salmon as are today the northern pacific coast rivers of Canada and Alaska with the famous runs of Sockeye and Chinook.

Salmo Salar (the Leaper). Sockeye Salmon leaping up Brook Falls, Katmai National Park, Alaska.

Some salmon fishers have tried to explain the apparent haphazard taking habits of salmon as being a variation in feeding suppression by different salmon; in other words, that some salmon are more ready takers than others depending on the different levels of feeding suppression or'anorexia' in the fish. I asked Allan Donaldson's opinion on this, and he pointed out that such an idea was impossible to prove either way, without tagging every fish in the river and seeing how many times certain tagged

Bahn Pool in early spring, River Carron. Even at this time of the year, the skimmed Collie Dog works well when retrieved square to the pool.

fish were caught. He thought it very unlikely that salmon physiology would differ in this way from one fish to another, and in any case, although a known fish in a lie might give the impression of being a poor taker by refusing a fly on one occasion, on another occasion under different fishing conditions the fish would take quite happily!

Allan told me a fascinating story of an occasion when he was standing on a bridge over the river Beauly in northeast Scotland, watching a group of salmon lying in clear water in a pool beneath the bridge. Quite unexpectedly, one of the salmon began to become agitated, flexing the pectoral fins, opening and closing its mouth and gills more obviously and flexing the tail from side to side. Then suddenly the salmon came up from its lie and swallowed an insect on the surface of the water. It then returned to the group of salmon and settled back

Looking up Bahn Pool from the tail, once again at a perfect height and with a good chance of some early spring salmon.

into its station. Something triggered that fish to suddenly come onto the feed, even though it was in fresh water, and since there was a hatch of flies on the water, my hunch would be that it was a rise in barometric pressure, coinciding with the sight of a food object floating overhead. I believe it must be the coinciding rise in barometric pressure that triggers the reflex feeding response.

Salmon fishers will know very well the many occasions when they can see their fly (the food) fishing across the pool, in clear water, right in front of salmon – but the salmon refuse to respond in any way at all – not even the flicker of a fin! The salmon needs to see the fly AND there needs to be the conditioned reflex to feed.

Then, under different fishing conditions, when the barometer is steady, the salmon will see the fly, follow it across the pool, but still not take it. We'll resort to skimming a Collie Dog across the surface and see the salmon splash at the fly, time and again, and sometimes we can actually see that the salmon's mouth is tight closed. There is clearly a slight feeding urge being triggered, but it is not strong enough to entice the salmon to actually grab the food on every occasion. This is the 'taking short' behaviour that can be so frustrating. This was very much our experience just three weeks ago in our spring 2005 fishing week on the Amat water of Glen Carron. We had a stable weather system and a stable barometer most of the week. The fish were often taking short, a higher percentage were hooked and lost than in the previous year, and many of those caught were hooked in the front of the mouth. On the day when Allan caught two salmon just as the barometer began to fall at 4.15 pm, I had fished hard through the morning (when the baro was still steady), raising six different fish to the Collie Dog. One salmon splashed at the fly in Vernons pool and followed it again across the pool to lunge at it again – but never took it and would not come again for the fly. After the double success at 4.15 pm, one on a size 10 Kylie shrimp (one of Allan's own patterns) the other thirty minutes later on a Collie Dog, Allan rose one more salmon in the Park pool in the evening, which also came short, and otherwise neither Allan (an exceptional salmon fisher) or the rest of the party had any further joy that day.

Chapter Five

When the chips are down

'There are charms made only for distant admiration'
Dr Johnson

Allan Donaldson proved that the odd fresh run salmon can be tempted on a slowly falling barometer and thankfully he has shared with us a charm that is not only for distant admiration. When the fishing conditions become difficult, Allan has absolutely mastered the skill of 'Collie skimming', and has kindly taught us it's magic. On a stable, and particularly on a falling barometer it is clearly necessary to induce a take, using methods that might be more likely to overcome a mood of suppressed feeding, and there are various well known approaches.

The head of the Long Pool, looking never better. A big holding pool for the Amat Estate waters of the Carron, and a joy to fish at any time of the year, but particularly the tail of the pool in a good height of water.

Probably the first thing to try is a change of fly size, either up or down, and even to go very small, despite cold water conditions. A size 10 (1.5 inches, including tail) in spring water temperatures of 52 degrees F was enough to induce a salmon to take in the Garvault pool for Allan on May 4th this year. Then 30 minutes later a second salmon grabbed his Collie Dog – fully four to five inches in length and skimming at speed over the surface of the water. One might be surprised by the length of the Collie Dog fly – 4 inches, and by its amazing success rate; but actually this fly is a superb imitation of the sand eel, and even the way the Collie Dog has to be fished is a replica of how the sand eel swims.

I have seen sand eels in the rock pools of Trebarwith beach in Cornwall, and to my amazement I noticed that they swim on the surface of the water exactly like a Collie Dog – forming a V in the surface film of the water, and you see the alternate flash of silver against the black of their backs. Salmon fishing is a fascinating challenge, but it is not illogical. Salmon go mad for the Collie Dog, if fished correctly, because it looks like the food they love to eat in the sea.

A cobalt beauty for Bill Auden at the head of the Long Pool. Bill caught this cracking 8¼lb spring salmon on 6th May 2004 at 19.50 on a Rising barometer.

Allan ties the Collie Dog on a one inch, or one and a half inch plastic tube with rear third left undressed, mid third lilac lurex and front third copper lurex, silver wire over the lurex. The wing is four to five inches of black goat hair with a few strands of lure-flash tied in. The pattern has been well known for years, but it is Allan's method of fishing the fly that makes all the difference. It is essential that the fly is cast square to the river and fished back over the surface in a smooth and rapid movement, perfectly square to the river, creating a V in the surface of the water. Sometimes the salmon follow the fly right to the bank below you, so the Collie Dog must be fished right to your feet. It is almost impossible to fish the fly too fast, and the resulting takes are absolutely thrilling. Sometimes the salmon will come out of the water and come down onto the fly, in a split second of purposeful feeding aggression. Sometimes they will continue to come short, and show interest in the fly by splashing at it, but not taking the fly. This is not a case of the fish missing the fly – if the salmon wants to grab the fly, it will. But when you see the salmon splashing at the fly with its mouth tightly shut, you can obviously see that the instinct to feed has been stimulated, but that the conditioned reflex is not sufficiently triggered to actually grab the food. As mentioned before, during the study, these occasions coincided with a stable or falling barometer. However, when fishing conditions are difficult and no salmon are moving to the conventional fly, 'Collie skimming' can be an exciting way to see salmon, when none are otherwise showing and eventually, with perseverance, the odd salmon will latch onto the fly.

A second successful pattern for this method of salmon fishing is the Sunray Shadow. This is also tied on a plastic tube, two thirds dressed with silver lurex and silver rib over. The wing is brown squirrel, some strands of peacock herl and black goat, also tied four inches long. Both the Collie Dog and Sunray Shadow can induce a take in tough conditions, but on a rising barometer they are deadly. The salmon take ferociously and are usually well hooked in the scissors. Fishing a long line across the head of the Long pool at Amat, during a prolific hatch of insects, a salmon took the Sunray Shadow at fully 25 yards and went completely 'stone mad', as Allan would say. The fish fought furiously for a few minutes, before shaking free and leaving me with a completely flattened treble! Indeed the problem is that in these excellent fishing conditions the salmon are so stimulated to feed that they can occasionally take the fly too deeply and there is a danger of damaging the gills.

At Amat we return all salmon if they are not damaged, so a fish bleeding from the gills is a disaster and although it happens very rarely we very much

Colette plays a big salmon, caught on the skimmed Collie Dog, at the head of the Long Pool, River Carron.

The smile says it all as Allan safely nets a 12lb salmon for Colette. Colette caught her salmon at 12.20 on 6th May 2004 on a Stable barometer.

regret having to kill the fish. The last salmon I was forced to kill was a salmon I caught on the 28th July 2000 in Bahn pool on Amat, River Carron. Although the water was low, the barometer was rising steadily and the salmon took the Sunray Shadow aggressively, swallowing the fly to the back of the mouth. On removing the fly, despite using fly forceps (an essential tool when you are endeavouring always to return salmon), I damaged the gills and had to kill the salmon. Fortunately, when the barometer is rising and we have those wonderful days when the conventional fly method can bring you those exquisite moments of solid pulls and well hooked fish, there is no need to resort to the Collie Dog or Sunray Shadow, and the danger of a damaged fish is consequently reduced. Allan Donaldson always recommends going through a pool with the conventional fly first before trying the Collie Dog.

Nothing like it in the world. The author has some fun with a salmon in the tail of the Long Pool in perfect water height.

Just about ready to celebrate! The author returns an 8 lb fresh springer to go on up-stream and make some more fresh springers! This one was caught on 6th May 2003 at 10.00 am on a Rising barometer.

The rather trying conditions of salmon 'taking short' were with us in early June 2003. I was kindly invited by Jamie Guise to join his party of fishers on the Carysville beat of the Blackwater in Ireland, sharing a rod with my father. Carysville can be prolific and this early June week combines the late spring run of salmon, which are often the largest fish, and the early grilse run. It is a most beautiful stretch of river, with perfect wading and ideal fly water. The river is wide enough to fish the pools simultaneously from both banks and this actually greatly adds to the pleasure, since you can watch your fellow fishers in action while keeping a fly in the water yourself. I had the pleasure of watching the expert overhead casting of Jamie Guise, punctuated by occasional plumes of cigar smoke, while following him down the Cabin pool, and also the Spey casting of Michael de Lotbiniere, who was fishing opposite me from the Key Wall.

George Andrews prepares to return a handsome 10 lb springer in Sandy's Pool, Amat, River Carron. George caught this one at 12.40 on 4th May 2004 on a Stable barometer.

For the last three days of the week, while I was with the party, the barometer was stable and the fishing conditions difficult. Some fish were coming to the fly, but few were hooked and fewer still landed. On Saturday morning my line finally went solid right at the end of the cast, while the fly was on the dangle, in the tail of the Top Flats, in very deep water. I never saw the fish. This was forever to be my 'one that got away' story. I'd never felt a weight like it – absolutely solid and moving with simple, slow and dogged determination straight down and across to the deepest part of that very deep pool. Knowing that the fish were taking short I was pretty sure this would be another fish just hooked in the kype, or the front of the mouth. On these occasions I favour giving the rod a damn good yank, upwards, to try and drive a hook that is probably only lightly embedded. I've never lost a fish in doing this as this action is done after the fish is actually 'on', there is at least twenty to thirty yards of line out to the fish, and the stretch in the line avoids any chance of a break.

This fish certainly felt like a monster and continued to circle around in deep water for about ten minutes, it never surfaced and never tore off up or down stream – just doggedly circled. It decided to come closer into the bank at my feet, but in very deep water, and suddenly the hook came free. I checked the points of my size eight Irish shrimp treble, they were razor sharp and neither bent nor damaged. I'm afraid I simply had to accept that this was yet another salmon that had taken short and been lightly hooked in the kype or front of the mouth. The part of the mouth that is very much harder than any other.

The Steps Pool and Campbell's Run at Amat, Glen Carron on a beautiful day in Scotland.

I fished on down and stepped into the head of Professors pool, and could see Edward Benson fishing the Cabin pool below, casting a long line and covering the water perfectly. Edward had only recently taken up salmon fishing, but, as with anyone determined to learn the skills and put in the time, Edward had quickly mastered the casting of a 15 foot salmon rod, and had caught several grilse – but not yet his first salmon. At last the moment finally came and Edward's efforts were rewarded. The reel sang out, and Edward lifted into his first salmon. Quickly, and with heart pounding, I reeled in and ran down to the bank beside him with my net. Netting someone's first salmon doesn't happen every day of the week and I was trying to keep as calm as possible. Edward showed great patience and, despite heart stopping runs back into mid-stream, he brought his fish safely to the net. The emotion immediately erupted into relief and elation as the fish was landed and we shook hands over a great occasion. Unlike the lame traveller, who is happy enough to see a mule on any occasion, the salmon fisher 'in extremis' might regard an untried companion with a net as a mixed blessing. Fortunately Edward was happy enough with me!

Early morning mist over the Careysville beat of the Blackwater in southern Ireland.

The fly, a size eight treble, was firmly hooked in the side jaw of the salmon and, having dispatched the fish, I asked Edward if he minded if I did a quick 'autopsy' on the salmon while it was still fresh. Edward had also suffered from fish 'taking short' that week, so was equally interested in the test. I took the treble and tried to embed two of the points into the kype of the salmon. No matter how hard I pulled, I could not get two points of the treble into the kype beyond the barb. In other words, if two points were hooked into the kype, or the front lower jaw of the fish, the fly might very well drop out unless there was exact and opposite pull to keep the hook in place. This was a pull that is obviously also weakened by twenty to thirty yards of stretch affected line. However, when I put just one point into the front of the jaw, although difficult, the point could be pulled into the fish beyond the barb – establishing a decent hold.

To get an idea of the true effect of stretch in the line over thirty yards, and to compare the hooking performance of trebles, doubles and singles I later tried striking each hook into a wine cork, hammered into a fence post.

For the purpose of a consistent test, I used a new Partridge treble, double and single salmon hook and tied each onto the six foot leader nylon with a double turle knot – so that the pulling angle was as it might be for the real thing. The distance from the rod tip to the cork was the same for each hook – exactly 25 yards, and for each hook, I gave the rod three good strikes, which might best imitate the setting of a hook and then perhaps some pulls from the fish. When the two points of a treble were pulled into the cork the points were not even embedded up to the barb. The single point of the treble was tested and would embed up to the barb, but not beyond it. The double hook also became embedded only up to the barb, but not beyond it, and would not have held if the line slackened. However, the single hook was embedded right up to the bend and well beyond the barb – providing by far the best hooking.

The single hook performed far better than the single hook of the treble, as the treble has a straight shaft from bend to eye, which is inclined to cantilever, whereas the single was a Partridge Bartleet Supreme with an arching shaft, which maintains a wide gape, but is designed to have the pulling force (from the eye of the hook) much more in line with the point of the hook – avoiding any cantilevering, and directing much more of the pulling force from the eye of the hook into the point of the hook.

From then on I have tied all my salmon flies on singles and use singles on tubes as well, losing far fewer fish. Allan Donaldson at Amat is also favouring singles these days. He began using single hooks when trebles were banned on the Kyle rivers of Sutherland two years ago, for easier catch

Looking down to the Sand Hole, one of the most prolific pools on the Careysville beat of the Blackwater.

and release, and found the hooking performance of a single was excellent. It was Allan who recommended the Partridge Bartleet hook, and from the way it was driven into a wine cork, right to the bend, I would recommend it to anyone. Obviously only half the force is required to drive a single as opposed to a double hook, so it all stands to reason! It also follows that a single hook with no barb, or with the barb pinched flat will be driven home even more easily, and the move to barbless hooks may even lead to more short-taking salmon being landed than is the case now.

Heady days

*'We cleansed our beards of the mutton grease,
We lay on our mats and were filled with peace'*

WHEN MEN AND MOUNTAINS MEET
H.W.Tilman

Happily, if you wait long enough, the rewards will come. *'Strenuousness is the path of true glory and sloth the way of death'*, as a proverbial guide might be putting it a bit strong, but there is no doubt that you have to put the hours in to catch salmon. Accepting, as I do, that a steadily rising barometer is the answer to our prayers does not mean that we wait until the barometer is rising before we potter out to the river with a fishing rod. We are looking for a rising barometer, and this can be something that can happen any time, and we need to be beside the river to take advantage of it. It does not matter if the barometer is low or high, it is the movement, up or down, that affects the behaviour of the trout and salmon – as can be seen in the study.

Obviously, when arriving at the lake or river for your week's fishing it is preferable to find the barometer low, and better still just after a tremendous downpour. This way you will have plenty of water, fresh fish arriving into your pools and the barometer rising – perfect! However, unfortunately this heady combination rarely coincides with the week we are booked on the river, and this is why catching salmon always appears like a walk in the park on some rare occasions, and damn nigh impossible on others! I have mentioned that a rising barometric pressure appears to be the final trigger to bring on the conditioned reflex of an impulse to feed, and for salmon and trout to take the fly or lure. But, obviously the many other well known factors need to be in place as well to provide a perfect day's fishing – good water height and temperature to encourage the fresh fish to run, and fresh fish coming into your pools. However, these elements are more frequently in place, and yet the fish still refuse to take; you need these factors AND at least a stable or, better still, a rising barometer.

Some friends of ours, the Remnants, Reynolds, Pecks and Mellys were fortunate enough to arrive at the river for their week's fishing with the conditions absolutely perfect. The occasion was early September 1992 and the river was the Fleet and its small tributary, the Carnaig, in Sutherland – not far north of the river Carron. After a substantial spate over the weekend, the river was at perfect height on Monday 7th September, when Hugo and Annabelle Remnant sallied forth with the ghillie to try their luck. Within a very short time they were both landing grilse and salmon in quick succession and it was clear that they were in for one of those truly amazing day's fishing. All the fish were fresh and they were taking size eight Yabbie and Ally's shrimp patterns – both tied with a long tail. All were well hooked and none were lost – the taking was so positive. The wonderful fishing continued on Tuesday 8th September, with Hugo himself landing five fish in just three hours from 10.45 am. In all, eleven salmon were caught in the day, with Simon Peck catching four, Annabelle Remnant another one, and Amanda Reynolds her first salmon. The action slowed in the late afternoon, and then on the Wednesday another eight salmon were caught, one on the Thursday and one on Friday. A total of 31 salmon and grilse, 1 sea trout and a slob trout were caught in the week, with 29 salmon and grilse caught on the first three days.

In an effort to try and confirm my theory that a fast rising barometer might explain the extremely positive taking of the salmon on these two days, I obtained the barometric readings for the 7th and 8th September 1992, from the nearest Met station, which is again Tain. Please refer to the graph for September 1992 at the end of this chapter. The readings clearly show the dramatic rise in barometric pressure on the 7th (6 mb from 7.00 am to 10.00 pm). The rise in pressure continues in the morning of the 8th (2.4 mb from 7.00 am to 1.00 pm), but then levels out to 1001 mb from 1.00 pm to 6.00 pm – all consistent with the fishing fortunes of the party on the Fleet and Carnaig in that memorable year. In fact, no other thirty eight hour period in the study compares with the amazing 18.8 mb rise in barometric pressure from 1.00 am on the 7th September until 3.00 pm on the 8th September – during which time 21 of the week's 31 salmon are caught! Heady days indeed! By the time Hugo and Annabelle began fishing at around 9.30 am on the 7th September there had been a rise of no less than 10.5 mb since 1.00 am in the morning! The piscatorial dinner gong had been sounding loudly for eight hours already!

Hugo Remnant particularly remarked to me that during the most prolific fishing periods the fly was taken right to the back of the mouth by the salmon and he did not lose a single fish. The taking behaviour changed after Wednesday morning as fish came less enthusiastically to the fly and the catch numbers fell away during the rest of the week, despite general fishing conditions apparently remaining favourable.

Hugh Falkus, perhaps one of the most experienced and observant salmon fishers of recent years, tried to explain this phenomenon of different taking behaviour in salmon. In chapter XIV, page 356, of his book 'Salmon Fishing' Falkus explains his notion, and he emphasises that it is just a 'notion', that salmon of different runs from the sea behave differently and in particular they take a lure differently, even if the runs are separated by as little as two tides, a matter of hours: Falkus is discussing why salmon might be lost after hooking;

'There will be exceptions, notably softness of flesh in very fresh-run fish, but certainly many losses must be due to the way in which the lure has been taken. As stated in Chapter II, the theory that fish always take a lure in the same way, I know from observation to be false. And that observation is heightened by what happens on the river bank. I have often noticed that different runs of salmon coming fresh from the sea, although separated by only a day, sometimes seem to display different looks and behavioural characteristics – to the extent, even, of preferring different lures; And, perhaps most significantly of all, they tend to **take** *differently. About the latter I am in no doubt. And in my experience it applies equally to different runs of sea trout, even though these runs may differ merely by a matter of hours – the time taken by the ebb and flow of a single tide. This is only an impression; a* **notion**. *But if it is true it goes some way towards explaining why on occasion there should be such a disparity in our success/failure rate when fish are lost for no apparent reasons.*

As an example; During a week in early spring on the river Dee, I caught five salmon on sunk fly in my first two days. These fish were all much of a size and shape. Typical fresh-run Dee springers, ranging from 7½ lb to 9 lb. Each fish had sucked the fly right into the back of his mouth; the hook so deep in the throat that it had to be recovered with artery forceps. During the next two days, in addition to having several pulls, I caught two fish but lost three. Those I landed were larger fish than hitherto: 17lb and 15 lb. They seemed a different stamp of salmon altogether, although just as fresh and with female tide lice on them. Each was **very lightly hooked**, *right in the front of the mouth. And remember, three more were hooked but came off. The following day was virtually unfishable owing to a sudden rise of water and tremendous gale force winds. I hooked and lost one fish on a spinner. On my last day I caught three more on the fly, each hooked as firmly as those earlier fish had been, the hook sucked right to the back of the throat so that, again, forceps were needed. And again, these fish were clearly members of a new run, each being 8-9 lb.*

This is the sort of pattern I have experienced on many occasions, both with salmon and sea trout, during the times of the year when the majority of fish were running. (I may say that, in the example given, all the fish were caught on a 3½ inch fly of exactly the same size and pattern – though of different weights to suit depth and current in the various taking lies.) Now I don't want to make too much of this. It is all rather tenuous stuff. But it is interesting, and I mention it because it may be the reason why on occasion we suffer those irritating runs of misfortune when fish after fish comes off. Also, (although in this case I used the same size and pattern of fly), it helps to explain why certain lures succeed on some days and not on others. Perhaps, most of all, it encourages us to think that if one lure fails it is worthwhile to try another; that in addition to boosting our confidence, there may really be a chance that this new offering will be preferred. I will take the matter no further than that - and repeat that it is just a notion. Nevertheless, it may offer solace to any unfortunate reader who has suffered an unaccountable and infuriating series of losses, or been puzzled why one fish he lands has the hook at the back of its throat, whereas with another fish, lightly hooked up front, the hook has fallen out on landing.' (Bold italics are Falkus's).

On this subject I quote Falkus in full because it shows that he also recognised that salmon taking behaviour is a fascinating phenomenon and one which he wished to explain somehow. He offers his theory, with some reservation, that the alternating taking behaviour may be explained by separate runs of salmon behaving differently and even appearing different – but in fact the probable answer indeed lies once again with barometric pressure.

In Falkus's week on the Dee we can see the classic evolution of barometric pressure, before and after rainfall, and the effects it is having on salmon taking behaviour. For the first two days, when the salmon are taking the fly to the back of the mouth, the barometer is obviously rising steadily, then a new weather front begins to interfere with conditions and for the next two days the barometer is either steady or beginning to fall, and the salmon are harder to catch and begin to take short, on the night of the fourth day no doubt the barometer falls sharply, and on the fifth day Falkus is greeted by a rising river and gale-force winds. That night the storm passes through and the barometer starts to rise again, providing excellent fishing conditions again on the sixth and final day when the salmon are taking with the same enthusiasm as with the rising barometer of the first two days, and the fly is once again sucked to the back of the throat.

Short taking salmon and sea trout will continue to exasperate from time to time, but if you are carrying a barometric watch you will have all the explanation you need for their strange taking behaviour. Hugh Falkus may have, in my opinion, underestimated the significance of barometric pressure in salmon and sea trout behaviour, but his remark concerning different weights of fly to suit water depth and current in the various taking lies is another piece of his huge experience that is thankfully shared with us.

The sixth sense

'The bleating of the kid excites the tiger'
Rudyard Kipling

If the fishing conditions look promising I might declare that it feels distinctly 'fishy', but no more than that. I do not spend enough time beside a river each year, sadly, to obtain what might be described as an innate 'feel' for the right moment to go fishing – the most likely time to entice a salmon to take. I do believe that some dedicated ghillies can obtain this refined instinct through many years spent beside a river, and many, many hours of watching salmon and fishing for them.

There must also be a few dedicated salmon fishers in the world who have re-learnt these natural 'hunting instincts' and the intuition that goes with spending many, many happy days fishing, and observing the behaviour of salmon and sea trout in all conditions and all elements of weather – almost by way of a life-time's dedication. Hugh Falkus and Arthur Ogelsby are both giants in modern salmon and sea trout fishing. They have written the definitive salmon and sea trout fishing books and have shared with the reader their every thought and experience regarding the habits of salmon and sea trout and how to catch them. In his chapter on 'The Feeling' Hugh Falkus, in 'Salmon fishing, A Practical Guide', discusses two incidents when he believed that he and Arthur Ogelsby, when fishing together, both independently decided that the moment to fish for a taking salmon had arrived. In the event, Falkus caught the fish just as Ogelsby arrived to give the salmon a go himself! On the second occasion Falkus describes a day with a storm brewing, but with no fish coming to the fly all morning. Suddenly Falkus gets the feeling that he will catch a taking fish in a certain pool on the Dee and, bringing the ghillie down to the pool, he set off and caught the fish precisely where and when he expected to. Just as the fish was landed the thunder, lightning and rain began to break.

After seeing the results of the study, and knowing from the Met Office that the onset of rain coincides with a rise in barometric pressure, and the onset of a thunder storm brings an even sharper rise in pressure, I wonder whether the 'feeling' that Falkus and Oglesby were experiencing was actually a rise in barometric pressure, and it is this rise (particularly the sharp rise just as a thunderstorm breaks) that gave them the intuition that the salmon were about to 'come on' to the take? Hugh Falkus himself cannot explain in his book what might be the reason for these 'feelings' but he is convinced that he occasionally has the intuitive knowledge of when to fish for salmon. After wearing a Casio barometric watch for seven years, I am beginning to associate certain weather systems and cloud formations, wind speeds and types, with barometric pressure movements up and down. While I am learning about weather and, using the watch, seeing how it is affected by barometric pressure changes, I suppose Hugh Falkus and Arthur Oglesby were instinctively learning about weather and the feelings they experienced with these changing conditions in relation to the moods of the salmon and sea trout. They spent enough time beside a river to have developed innate hunting instincts. But for me, spending just twelve days a year on a salmon river, I'm sure I will always need a barometric watch!

Fly selection and depth

'The crows are searching for the wind'
Jimmy Ewen

On a river that you know well, you can make an educated guess. You can dip a finger in the river and get a feel of the temperature, you can take a look at the river and it's height, hold up the fly on the end of your line and say to yourself – too damn big, or… a mite too small – change the fly and away you go. But, on water that you do not know, or are visiting for the first time, there needs to be the odd yard-stick. Thankfully there may be a ghillie or local guide to give advice, but in the absence of that, there is still a correlating size table that can help:

SALMON FLY SIZE INDICATOR
FOR DIFFERENT WATER CONDITIONS

Three different water conditions:

1	River height HIGH	River speed FAST	River water CLEAR
2	River height AVERAGE	River speed AVERAGE	River water CLEAR
3	River height LOW	River speed AVERAGE	River water CLEAR

Water Temperature in

Degrees Fahrenheight(°F)	Degrees Centigrade(°C)	Water Condition	Tube Size (Inches)	Fly Hook Size
34-35°	2°	**1**	2½	
		2	2	
		3	1¾	
36-37°	3°	**1**	2	
		2	1¾	
		3	1¾	
38-39°	4°	**1**	2	
		2	1¾	
		3	1½	
40-41°	5°	**1**	1¾	
		2	1½	
		3	1¼	
42-43°	6°	**1**	1½	2/0
		2	1¼	2
		3	1¼	2
44-45°	7°	**1**	1½	1/0
		2	1¼	2
		3	1	4
46-47°	8°	**1**	1¼	2/0
		2	1	2
		3	1	4

Degrees Fahrenheight(°F)	Degrees Centigrade(°C)	Water Condition	Tube Size (Inches)	Fly Hook Size
48-49°	9°	1	1¼	2
		2	1	4
		3	1	6
50-51°	10°	1	1	4
		2	1	6
		3	¾	6
52-53°	11°	1	1	4
		2	¾	6
		3	¾	8
54-55°	12°	1	1	6
		2	¾	8
		3	¾	8
56-57°	14°	1	¾	6
		2	¾	8
		3	¾	10
58-59°	15°	1	¾	8
		2	¾	10
		3	½	10
60-61°	16°	1	¾	8
		2	½	10
		3	½	12
62-63°	17°	1	¾	10
		2	½	12
		3	½	12
64-65°	18°	1	½	10
		2	½	12
		3	½	12
66-67°	19°	1	½	10
		2	½	12
		3	½	14
68-69°	20°	1	½	12
		2	½	14
		3	½	14

If the water is dirty, such as after a spate, add ½ inch of tube size or two fly sizes in water temperatures between 34 to 45° F, and in water temperatures between 46 to 69° F then add ¼ inch of tube size and one fly size.

The suggested Tube Size for each water condition and temperature is the actual length of the tube. The wing is usually tied long enough to cover the hook, but in temperatures over 60° F the wing may advisably be tied shorter, simply to cover the length of the tube, and more sparsely. The beauty of tubes is that the appropriate length for the water condition can be maintained, but the weight can be adjusted to suit the depth of the water – alternating between brass, aluminium and plastic tubes to find the level at which the salmon are lying.

The book has so far sought to explain why and when salmon will take a fly after they enter fresh water. The fact that salmon take different sized flies and lures in different heights of river and at different water temperatures is a well known phenomenon, but is, on the face of it, no less mystifying. As mentioned earlier, salmon behaviour is truly fascinating, but it is not illogical; and for me the question of water height and temperature and the coinciding fly size that salmon will take is very simply explained. Once again, I believe it must be reflex conditioning. When the water is high the fish are presented with feeding conditions reminiscent of the sea, the same applies when the water is cold, and all the more so when both conditions apply. In the sea the salmon are feeding on prey that is larger (small fish such as capelin, sprats, young cod and whiting; and sand eels, prawns, small squid etc) than the prey on which they fed in the river as parr and smolts – tiny insect larvae, freshwater shrimp, beetles etc.

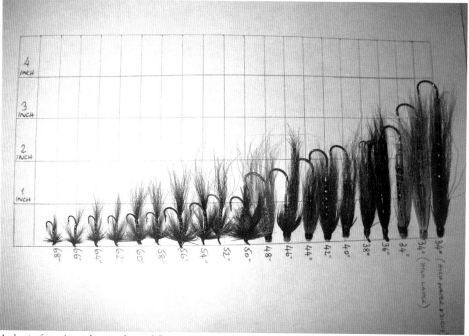

A chart of varying salmon tube and fly sizes suitable for different water temperatures.

When the river is running at normal height the salmon would, I believe, be inclined to associate feeding with their fresh water feeding as parr and smolts. When the water warms up and when the river height is low, the association to fresh water feeding is increasingly enhanced and the salmon take ever smaller flies, and can eventually be caught on very small flies indeed in the warmest water conditions. The parr and smolts would have also experienced the rivers in very cold winter conditions – down to 34 degrees F, but in these conditions the feeding would be very sparse, and the main feeding for young parr and smolts would be as the river warms up, in the spring, to 45 degrees F when the insect activity begins – becoming more prolific as the water warms to the summer temperatures of 60-65 degrees F. Just as the strength of the conditioned feeding response of salmon to the rising barometer is linked to the steepness of the rise in barometric pressure, so the conditioned feeding response of the salmon to the type of prey (in terms of size) is linked to the strength of the triggering conditions in terms of water height and temperature.

Unfortunately it is not possible to prove this explanation for fly size, but I like it as a theory because it seems entirely logical! If you accept, as I do, that salmon take a fly in fresh water in response to a conditioned reflex to feed (rather than from annoyance or curiosity), then the salmon, when they feed, must also surely be conditioned to those environmental conditions in which they find certain types and sizes of food. The fact that in warmer water and lower river heights the salmon simply take smaller sizes of the same fly pattern that might be successful in colder and higher river conditions is also not surprising – they all imitate food. Small trout flies such as the Black Pennell, the Black and Peacock Spider and the Soldier Palmer have been successful for me with the late summer salmon on South Uist in the Scottish Outer Hebrides; and each, in its own way, is imitating prey on which the salmon would have fed as a parr and smolt – the Black Pennell, an emerging nymph pattern, the Black and Peacock, a caddis larvae and the Soldier Palmer, a freshwater shrimp. The half-inch tube flies and size twelve or fourteen Stoats Tails are also catching salmon in 66 degrees F summer temperatures, whilst the same pattern in a one and a half inch brass tube will catch salmon in the cold spring waters of 40 degrees F.

The traditional trout wet fly patterns may certainly approximate what the salmon actually fed on in fresh water as parr and smolts, and as such they are every bit as likely to catch salmon in warmer conditions as the size 12 and 14 Stoat Tail and Willie Gun patterns. Actual nymph imitations may do well in the very warm conditions when a fly size of fourteen or sixteen becomes the necessary size, but for my money the key is not necessarily the imitation of fresh water insects, which would have been the staple diet of the young salmon, but the closest possible approximation to the food that the salmon will most readily remember and recognise and this can be

Some of the marine invertebrates that Atlantic salmon feed upon at sea; squid, euphausiid shrimp, amphipods, and copepods; all of which respond to barometric pressure change.

anything from a Hares Ear or Pheasant Tail nymph imitation to a shrimp pattern such as Ally's shrimp, Kylie shrimp or Yabbie, a fish pattern, such as Willie Gun or Stoats Tail or the sand eel patterns – the Collie Dog or Sunray Shadow. In short, as long as the fly approximates in both colour and shape the food on which the salmon or sea trout may have at some point fed, then size is the next triggering element. Salmon parr are very often only too happy to latch onto our size 14 flies, and this has always encouraged me to believe the adult grilse or salmon will also favour the pattern. In his book 'Salmon Fishing' Hugh Falkus pays tribute to L.R.N Gray who gave him the knowledge, in his own book 'Torridge Fishery', concerning fishing the upstream nymph for summer salmon:

'For several years past I have had much better results with salmon just before dusk on summer evenings by fishing for them, exactly as if they were large trout, with weighted nymphs. Sawyer's Pheasant Tail and Ivan's Green Nymph, tied on sea-trout hooks, have been successful instead of normal salmon and sea-trout flies fished down and across in the ordinary way. When our salmon have been trapped in a long, slow pool by several weeks of summer drought, they become hard to approach

unless the surface is rippled…an upstream nymph is sometimes the only chance'.

(I can't help but point out again that the best quoted time being *'just before dusk on summer evenings'*, the time, as already mentioned, when the barometer rises after the day time 'Heat Low', and the insects hatch).

For these very warm, low water, summer salmon fishing conditions, Falkus himself favours his own 'Dee Special Nymphs', dressed short on quarter or half inch brass tubes or on a tiny weighted treble hook. Black stoats tail with a little blue or yellow. Falkus writes *'when sunk deep and fished with a nymph-like action – a technique familiar to most trout anglers (sink and draw) – this little fly seems to induce salmon to have a go, and although my experience of using it is not great it has caught me a number of fish I would not otherwise have hooked. It has done so, moreover, in difficult conditions of high summer, with fish lying doggo in the pools'.*

The other important factor with salmon flies and tubes is the element of movement, and this is well understood by the modern salmon fly tier. By discerning the 'modern' salmon fly from the traditional, one is

My two salmon fly patterns; Captain Scarlet on the left and the Yabbie on the right. The Captain Scarlet is with tail of red 'ibis' and long fibres of orange bucktail, body of orange 'seal' fur and gold oval tinsel rib, cheeks of golden pheasant tippets, red 'ibis' wing, red cock hackle with hen badger hackle over. The Yabbie is with a long tail of fine soft red goat hair or squirrel, body of red floss and oval silver tinsel rib, wing and throat of orange squirrel tied to the bend and hackle of badger hen.

principally referring to hair wing patterns as opposed to the feather wing patterns that were so popular in the late 19th century (The Jock Scott, Thunder and Lightning etc).

I believe it was Hugh Falkus who first made the hair wing patterns popular in Britain in the 1970s, and they have continued to be successful since then because, as 'attractors', they are superior due to their lively movement in the water. I believe colour is also important in triggering the feeding response and it is not by accident that the successful flies are coloured red, yellow, orange and black – imitating Atlantic prawns; yellow, black and brown – imitating the shrimp; silver, green and black – imitating fish; and the obvious black and silver imitation of the sand eel – the Collie Dog. Many other combinations catch fish, and they all have the common denominator – they all have a shape and colour that imitates food that salmon have fed on to a greater or lesser extent.

Oceanic krill, the *euphausiid prawn*. As the prawns migrate to shallower depths on a rising barometer (usually observed in the evenings), they become available to the pelagic surface feeders, including the Atlantic salmon. The red colour is a carotenoid pigment, which is non-reflective to bioluminescent light (light produced by some deep-sea fish to hunt prey) and therefore acts as a camouflage in the deep depths. However under natural light the red and orange colours are very well seen by salmon and other surface feeders.

Allan Donaldson's phenomenally successful fly, the Kyley Shrimp. Tag of silver wire, tail of sparse orange bucktail and strands of orange twinkle, GP red breast feather over, butt of black floss, rear body of flat copper tinsel, rib of silver wire, central hackle of orange cock, front body of black floss, front false hackle of orange cock above and below, blue guinea fowl as throat, long jungle cock wings, with over-wing of orange cock hackle fibres and the head is with red varnish.

In imitating the real thing, the fly or tube must use any material that gives it authentic movement and life in the water. Seal fur bodies and soft hair materials such as goat, or marabou can help the impression of movement, and some fly tiers like the lureflash and the jungle cock eyes. The pattern that has caught me more salmon than any other is my own pattern, the Yabbie. This incorporates the long red goat hair tail, the red floss body with oval silver rib, orange squirrel for wing and throat, tied to the bend, and hen badger hackle to give wonderful movement to the whole fly, and encouraging sideways waggle in the water as it hangs in the current. It was originally designed as a shrimp imitation, but does look very much like a small squid in the water as well. Apparently, salmon also feed on small squid and this may account for the fly's success. Salmon have excellent vision and will chase a small fly from many yards away across a pool, and surely it cannot now be disputed that salmon see colour – the fact that they adopt spawning colours would be sufficient proof of the importance of colour to salmon in attracting a mate. I believe also that salmon are highly discerning. If the fly is not swimming in an authentic way, if hair from the tail is twisted around the bend of the hook, or if there is any weed attached at all, then the salmon will not take. It definitely pays to check the fly regularly, as Allan Donaldson advises *"they don't like it wi' salad"*!

Essentially, it's perfectly reasonable to expect a salmon or grilse to be every bit as fastidious in its taste for fly pattern as the wild rainbow or brown trout. They are, of course, related and the only thing that immediately separates them is the habitat in which they live. The salmon spends most of its time at sea, feeding on a huge variety of prey, and it seems perfectly reasonable that, like the trout, the salmon can be expected to be attracted to the closest possible imitations – no matter what they might be.

The euphausiid shrimp, *Thysanopoda monocantha.* Dr Jens Christian Holst, of the Bergen Institute of Marine Research, gave a speech in 2005 at the Fishmongers' Hall, describing how data storage tags from caught salmon have shown that salmon at sea will occasionally dive to depths of 140 m. The Atlantic salmon is a relatively shallow pelagic marine feeder, but the desire to feed on these deep sea prawns and shrimps as they migrate to the surface on a rising barometer may account for these recorded depths of 140 m.

We can be much more adventurous in our salmon fly dressing, because there's no telling what weird and esoteric creature the salmon of that particular river might have a preference for when they are feeding in their particular feeding grounds at sea. This perhaps explains why so many different colours and shapes of salmon fly will be successful in the different rivers and lakes of the world where we find salmon, and no doubt, of course, the same also goes for the sea trout. I once had the pleasure of watching a Canadian fisher play a Steelhead in a beautiful river in the north of Vancouver Island. This was an immensely strong fish and the fisher was using a single handed nine or ten foot rod. After about ten minutes the chap called

Three more deadly looking Kyley shrimps from the Donaldson stable – easily mistaken for the real thing!

up to me in the pool above, and I made my way down to help – arriving just in time to take the rod as he cradled the fish in mid-stream and removed the hook. I took a picture of this magnificent fish, which must have been around eight or nine pounds, and then the fish was returned – splashing us both as it raced away through the shallows up-stream.

The Canadian fisher was so elated and so grateful that I had been able to help him that he gave me the deadly fly that had done the damage. To my amazement, into my outstretched hand was plonked the most ugly looking creation I had ever seen. It was nothing more than a hook with some purple tinsel wrapped around it and a miserable little tail of the same sort of stuff that you might chuck over a Christmas tree. It's name was 'The Purple Bomber' and the Canadian handed it over with such reverence it might have been the Crown Jewels, or otherwise the last of its kind in his fly box. Unfortunately, the Purple Bomber did not produce the goods for me, but perhaps this was because I did not have much faith in it, and in my experience I believe you should always fish with the fly you most believe in at the time (as Jimmy Ewen advised – whichever fly you feel 'comfortable' with). In any case the point of the story is that the handsome Steelhead that grabbed that fly did not take it because it thought it looked like a Christmas

Euphausiid shrimp, *Thysanopoda microphthalma,* caught at a depth of 100 m in the N.E Atlantic. The varying colours of these shrimps, a major food source for Atlantic salmon, must surely explain the different colour combinations that produce successful salmon flies. Length approximately 1½ inches.

A fully dressed Kyley on a 1/0 Bartleet single hook - the true traditional dressing, by Allan Donaldson.

decoration – it grabbed it because, no matter how unlikely it may seem, it looked like something it had been gobbling up with great gusto at sea.

As a definitive author of reference on salmon and sea trout fishing, Hugh Falkus can hardly be beaten, and once again in his book, 'Salmon Fishing', he has ascertained and provided on Plate 2 the actual photographed live appearance of the crustaceans believed to be commonly eaten by salmon at sea. The euphausiid, Meganyctiphanes is a shrimp like crustacean, appearing green, brown and yellow, and partially translucent, and an inch or so in length; the prawn, Parapandulus richardii has a pink and translucent white appearance and the eggs it carries under the abdomen are deep crimson; the deep sea prawn, Acanthephyra sp., is 2-3 inches in length and is a vivid red, but appears black when at depths beyond the reach of daylight. It is comforting therefore to know that the shrimp patterns we have designed for salmon fishing (probably more by chance!) are indeed a close imitation of the sea going shrimp and prawn, and not of the boiled 'crevettes' that land on our plates with a slice of lemon. Orange, red, black and white colours work well, because they are present in the real thing.

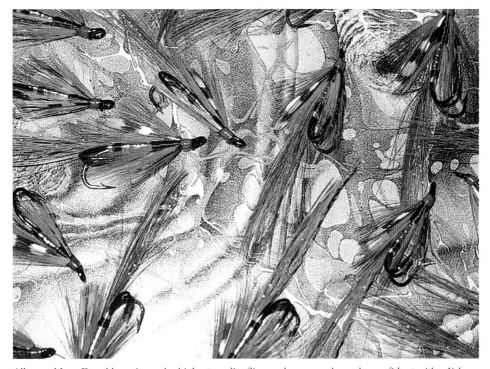

Allan and Jean Donaldson tie up the highest quality flies, and you can always be confident with a Kyley.

Stan Headley's book 'Salmon Flies of Scotland' gives many other shrimp patterns with greater or lesser predominance to yellows or even purples. Either you believe that colour matters or you don't, and my preference is for it being as important as fly size. Anecdotes abound of incidents when a change of fly colour has provided results, and most salmon fishers eventually settle on two or three patterns, which they know will succeed for them under any conditions encountered.

It occurs to me that light in the sea creates or enhances the elements of colour in the fish and crustaceans that make up a salmon's diet and while the depths at which these food sources are found will invariably be constantly changing, so will their colours – as with the deep sea prawn, from vivid red to jet black. We know from John Blaxter's studies on crustaceans that increasing barometric pressure will cause aquatic invertebrates to move towards the light. Such is the complexity of the sea going salmonid, Salmo Salar, it may also be possible to suggest that they

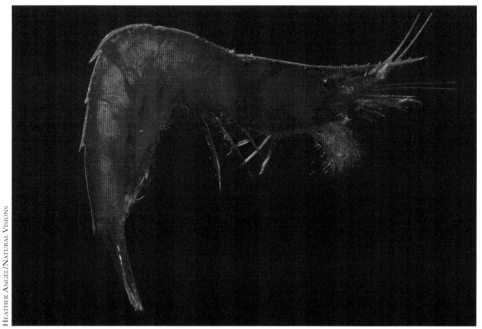

A red deep sea mesopelagic prawn, *Acanthephyra pelagica*, caught in the N.E Atlantic at 500 m depth. It is known that Atlantic salmon feed on this species. It lives at 1000 m depth by day and migrates up towards the surface in the evenings on a rising barometer. At the shallower depths, the salmon can feed on the deep sea mesopelagic prawn. Length approximately 2 – 3 inches, the red colour is created by carotenoid pigments. These pigments are stored within the fat and muscles of the salmon and released at the time of breeding to produce the handsome mating colours, particularly of cock fish.

associate the rising barometric pressure not only with hatching insects as young parr and smolts, but also with the appearance of amphipods and decapods in the sea, the shrimps and prawns, as they ascend towards the light on a rising barometric pressure. In the high latitudes of the North Atlantic, the summer months provide twenty four hour daylight by which the pelagic salmon can feed on deep-sea shrimps and prawns as they make their diurnal migration to the surface.

This may also perhaps account for the otherwise inexplicable proverb that bright flies do well on bright days and dull flies on overcast days, possibly replicating the bright colours in the prey at sea on sunny days, feeding close to the surface, and then the darker colours of the prey when feeding deeper or when it is overcast. It follows, therefore, that as a steady fall in barometric pressure indicates a need for deeper fishing, so too does it indicate a switch to a darker

The resemblance of Allan Donaldson's Kyley tubes to the mesopelagic prawn is uncanny and no wonder that fishers on the Carron in spring are clamouring for another of his 2 inch brass tubes with a 2½ inch hair wing! It's a deadly fly when the conditions are right, and hardly surprising!

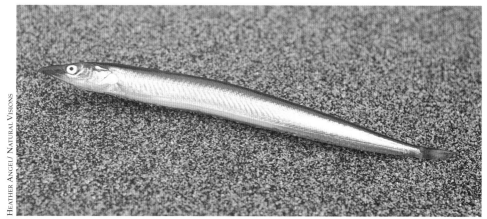

The greater sand eel, *Ammodytes lanceolatus*. Very probably top of the menu for salmon and sea trout. They can grow to ten inches, but commonly they are around four to six inches in length.

The Collie Dog fly – tied by Allan Donaldson in varying lengths. It is as much the V shape made in the surface film, on retrieve, that attracts the fish - without this 'V' in the surface the salmon are definitely less interested.

coloured fly. A rising barometer appears to bring the fish to the surface and this would sensibly imply a switch to a brighter coloured fly, especially if the conditions are sunny, always in an effort to trigger that reflex feeding response.

The sand eels, that I mentioned seeing on a Cornish beach, are black and silver when it is over-cast, but when caught in full sunlight the sand eels are transformed to an iridescent green and sparkling silver – much more resembling the Sunray Shadow pattern with strands of peacock herl.

Salmon are relatively shallow feeders at sea and if young cod, whiting and sprats are chasing the primary food in the food chain, the invertebrates, into shallower water then one would imagine that a rising barometer is even more indelibly imprinted into the reflex conditioning of a salmon. I've mentioned Jimmy Ewen's great remark about the crows, searching for the wind, prior to a storm, and I'm sure that ornithologists will certainly maintain that birds can sense barometric pressure change. But I wouldn't mind betting that sea birds are particularly sensitive in this respect.

As a boy of twelve years I was lucky enough to visit the bird sanctuary of Handa, an island off the north west coast of Scotland. There we would watch the graceful gannets and the comical puffins, razorbills and guillemots as they plunged into the sea to feed on capelin, Mallotus villosus, and sand eels, Ammodytes lanceolatus. I wondered at the time why the capelin didn't simply dive deeper to avoid the feeding frenzy from the birds. The capelin are themselves feeding on the small invertebrates in the sea that have been brought to the surface by a rising barometer, and no doubt the sea birds equally associate this rising barometer with shoals of capelin close to the surface.

If it is true that salmon associate feeding conditions at sea with barometric and hydrostatic pressures and that these pressures may indicate to the salmon at what depth they should be lying in order to find food, then it may follow that barometric pressure is indeed affecting the depth that salmon will lie in the pools within the rivers and along the shorelines of the lakes. The empirical evidence is that salmon show far less in the pools when the barometer is falling, and as physosternatous fish with open swim bladders they would need to surface far less to refill the air bladder through the mouth. They may also take up a deeper station as a reflex condition to their behaviour at sea when the barometer is falling. It is not impossible for both explanations to be valid. But from a practical point of view it is obviously well to know what is happening when the salmon apparently disappear.

Another salmon can't resist one of Allan's enticing Collie Dogs, skimmed across the pool, and to indicate the amazing length of the fly, Allan took this photo before safely returning the salmon.

As earlier mentioned, Hugh Falkus, amongst many other experts, recommends finding the salmon at whatever depth it may be lying, and I very much agree with this. A falling barometer seems to send the salmon deeper and from the study we also know that it is harder to bring the salmon to the fly while the barometer is falling. It is crucial to be flexible in the use of sink tip, intermediate or sinking fly lines to try and find the depth that the salmon are lying. When the conditions are difficult on a stable or even falling barometer, I believe the salmon and sea trout are less likely to rise to a surface fly and it is well worth bringing the fly closer to the fish. In trying to find the fish it is worth increasing the weight of the fly, but also sticking to the same appropriate length regarding water temperature; for the faster and deeper water of the pools, and even for very deep sections it must be worth trying a size larger as well. But with use of either different sized flies or of plastic, aluminium and brass tubes, and with the use of different fly lines, it is possible to achieve a good fly speed across any piece of water at depths that will find even the most elusive salmon. If, in some parts of a pool, this means some hand lining, then this method would also be appropriate.

If the depth you are fishing at, whether in spring, summer or autumn, is not producing results and if it is possible to fish deeper still, and if the barometer is stable or particularly if it is falling, then fish deeper still. A matter of an inch or two in depth can make the difference in inducing a take when the fish are hard to come by. I strongly believe that depth is every bit as important as fly size and pattern or colour, and I'm quite sure that most salmon and sea trout fishers recognise that too. But to keep the idea of the depth of your fly in the water as a constantly moving feast that needs to be frequently assessed in the light of conditions (particularly barometric pressure movements) is quite a discipline, but a discipline that adds to the thrill of the chase, and has for me brought great dividends since better understanding the importance of the barometer.

Releasing salmon, and salmon conservation

Baloo teaches Mowgli the Hunting Call:
'Give me leave to kill here because I am hungry';
and the answer is:
'Kill then for food, but not for pleasure'.

THE JUNGLE BOOK
Rudyard Kipling

'At 9.30 a.m. we commenced the ascent of the couloir leading from the nameless glacier to a point on the ridge, just to the east of Les Bans. So far the route had been nothing more than a steep grind in an angle where little could be seen, but now views opened out in several directions, and the way began to be interesting. It was more so, perhaps, to us than to our companion M.Reynaud, who had no rest in the last night. He was, more-over, heavily laden. Science was to be regarded – his pockets were stuffed with books; heights and angles were to be observed – his knapsack was filled with instruments; hunger was to be guarded against – his shoulders were ornamented with a huge nimbus of bread, and a leg of mutton swung behind from his knapsack, looking like an overgrown tail. Like a good-hearted fellow, he had brought this food, thinking we might be in need of it. As it happened, we were well provided for, and having our own packs to carry, could not relieve him of his superfluous burdens, which, naturally, he did not like to throw away. As the angles steepened, the strain on his strength became more and more apparent. At last he began to groan. At first a most gentle and mellow groan; but as we rose so did his groans, till at last the cliffs were groaning in echo, and we were moved to laughter.'

The first passage of the **Col De La Pilatte**, French Alps June 1863.

SCRAMBLES AMONGST THE ALPS
Edward Whymper

An amusing parable, really, for the salmon fisher who can't resist taking yet one more salmon. The Victorian era in which Edward Whymper was making his brilliant impact as a climber in the Alps, and eventually making the first ascent of the Matterhorn in 1865, was indeed an era of excess. The indulgence with which M. Reynaud was approaching his Alpine climbing experience was quite common, and the same excess and indulgence was absolutely commonplace in the worlds of hunting, shooting and fishing. We know, of course, how the tigers were shot out in India, the big game in Africa; how the wild grouse and partridge shoots in Britain were badly over-exploited and how the rarer game birds such as Cappercaillie and Black Cock are now almost extinct in Scotland. Unfortunately the same applied to the salmon. In the late 19th and early 20th century the sheer numbers of salmon could cope with the huge rod catches, but when pollution and then sea netting of salmon started to take its toll in the post war period, the persisting Victorian and Edwardian approach to game fishing became truly devastating.

A pre-lunch catch for two rods on the Pvera river in Iceland, July 1933.
Fifty-five salmon on fly and worm. Captain A. Wenner and his brother wrote to Hardy Bros. to thank them for the excellent performance of their Hardy rods, reels, lines and fly patterns which accounted for seventy-seven salmon in the day, weighing a total of 847 lbs - a fair load for three pack horses.

It wasn't until the 1920's and '30's that a more sympathetic approach to mountaineering was adopted, and even then it was by just a few young adventurers who understood that the key to success in the natural environment was to make as little impact as possible and to travel light. H.W.Tilman and E.Shipton pioneered this respectful and highly successful low-key, lightweight, involvement with remote and unexplored regions of the greater mountain ranges of the world and their experience encouraged future expeditions to adopt the same methods – leading to the modern lightweight expeditions that *'leave only footprints and take only memories'.*

Thankfully the equivalent practice is at last appearing on the British salmon rivers – leaving only footprints and taking only memories. However, the Victorian 'sporting' principle of hunting to kill has been a hard one to lay to rest and the spring salmon have been particularly damaged by the refusal, until very recently, to return salmon – to 'catch and release'.

Whymper later describes how their party, during the descent, are only able to overcome a severe mountaineering obstacle by, literally, a leap of faith. M.Reynaud makes the leap across the gaping crevasse, rucksack, leg of mutton and all, *'and then we heard a thud as if a bundle of carpets had been pitched out of the window. When set upon his feet he was a sorry spectacle; his head was a great snowball; brandy was trickling out of one side of the knapsack, chartreuse out of the other – we bemoaned its loss, but we roared with laughter'*.

Mountaineers and fishers at the very least share an appreciation of strong refreshments, and excess in this respect is perhaps more forgivable, but as ever these things are best appreciated when they are proportionate, and sadly the Victorians littered the Alpine peaks with discarded bottles, so little did they respect or understand the environment. In the same way, the very word 'proportionate' seems to have escaped the minds of British salmon fishers for a few years too many, and largely, perhaps, from this sense of Victorian and Edwardian precedence.

Fishers of all the other fly-fishing Continents, not burdened by the historical mind-set, have been returning trout, sea trout and salmon for decades already. Rules of catch and release do differ from river to river, but the principles of conserving stock for future generations has been accepted and nurtured from Alaska to Tierra del Fuego, throughout New Zealand and Australia and in South Africa. Catch and release with barbless hooks applies on the great salmon rivers of Northern Russia.

In my game book I note that it was in 1994 that Jonny Shaw, on the Amat Estate in Sutherland, first introduced voluntary catch and release in the river Carron. His strong belief was that no salmon or grilse was more valuable than the ones that had made it back into the river to breed, that had survived the rigours of netting and seal predation and of decimation of their feeding grounds to return to the river of their birth in order to spawn a new generation. This crucial understanding of the need to preserve the Carron river stock was no less important since Jonny fully appreciated that the particular strain of salmon that is found in the Carron river is specially evolved and therefore suited to negotiating the steep falls along the length of the river. The photographs of the Carron salmon in this book, all of which are fish that were returned, clearly show the shallow depth of the salmon and grilse and their ideal 'torpedo' shape for better tackling the steep waterfalls. Salmon of the Tay differ again in shape, as do the salmon of the Tweed, Dee and Spey.

Playing a salmon mid-stream at the tail of the Long Pool, Amat, River Carron.

More importantly, Jonny Shaw refused to accept the widely peddled notion that salmon and grilse die of disease, or spread disease if they have been handled during catch and release. Long after other fly-fishing nations had proven that catch and release, if followed carefully, caused no fish losses whatsoever, the British rivers were still hanging onto misguided myths; and when you understand that Jonny Shaw on the Amat Estate was the first in Sutherland and probably the first in Scotland to introduce voluntary catch and release in 1994, you know how very late have been the proprietors of British salmon fisheries to fully understand the concept, compared to accepted practices overseas.

Thankfully, in 1996, all the Kyle of Sutherland salmon rivers agreed to introduce a catch and release scheme that aimed at a minimum of 85% of all salmon and grilse being returned, and until now this level has been achieved. The result has been ever improving numbers of fish returning to the rivers, and in particular improving spring runs. The year of 2004 (a possible three breeding cycles since the introduction of voluntary catch and release in 1994) produced an all time record catch on the Amat Estate on the river Carron. In this period not one single salmon has died due to catch and release – such an event would be immediately reported by ghillies on the river.

Another interesting bonus to the catch and release policy is that larger fish have been seen in the Carron river system in recent years, and the probable answer is that the fish that have been released in previous years have successfully spawned, returned to sea, spawned again one more time,

Always a hairy moment – organising the net to be ready for an orderly landing of the fish, and usually the moment when all hell breaks loose!

Best practice is to remove the hook while the fish is in the net, and in the water, but failing that, if the fish lies in a knotless net on the bank for a few moments to have the hook removed and a photo taken, no harm is done.

A very strong 10 lb bar of silver for the author in the Tail of Long Pool at 12.45, 6th May 2004, on a Stable barometer.

If you intend to return the salmon, it is important to keep the fish horizontal at all times, and to hold the salmon in the current for as long as it takes to revive the fish. If the fish is landed relatively quickly and returned without delay, the revival time is usually under a minute, and especially so for fresh run springers.

returned to sea, and come back as monsters! Not only have twenty pound plus salmon been seen in the river in the last two years, but some are being caught, and released, as well. It was fitting that the biggest of them all should be caught by Allan Donaldson himself. As ghillie on the Amat Estate, Allan has done more than anyone I know to promote, encourage and teach the correct methods for catch and release, and on the last day of the 2002 season a 33 lb Cock salmon rose to his size 10 kylie shrimp in no more than a foot of water and tore off down the Vernons pool. It is an epic tale of how he managed to land this enormous fish on no more than 8 lb nylon, entirely alone and with the light fast disappearing on the last day of September. Thankfully Allan managed to take a self-timed photograph, before returning the fish, and he has kindly given me a copy for this book.

A huge cock salmon for Allan Donaldson in the head of Vernons on Amat, River Carron. This 33lb salmon took Allan's size 10 Kyley Shrimp in the final throes of the last day of the season 2003, and was landed as darkness fell.

The spectacular mating colours are the result of a wonderful natural irony. The carotenoid pigments that produce this handsome display are derived from the deep-sea prawns and shrimps that use this same pigment as camouflage against their deep-sea predators. (Source: Dr. Richard Shelton, Research Director of the Atlantic Salmon Trust, in 'The Longshoreman').

The river Carron in Sutherland is proving that catch and release does dramatically improve the overall numbers of returning salmon and grilse. The Salmon and Trout Association, supported by the Fishmongers' Company, is working hard with many interested parties, including the Association of Salmon Fishery Boards, and organisations throughout Britain to try and preserve and improve British salmon, sea trout and trout stocks; and with growing acceptance of catch and release as well as reductions in netting at sea, the future of salmon and sea trout is looking brighter. The S & TA is also combating the Irish drift net fishery, which is damaging salmon and sea trout stocks not only in Ireland, but also the stocks of rivers in England and Wales, where efforts are being made to rejuvenate numbers of fish. Through their involvement with the North Atlantic Salmon Conservation Organisation, the S & TA have been able to put pressure on the Irish Government and to lobby the European Union Fisheries Delegation. There are now signs that the European Union will intervene to bring the Irish Government into line on the management and conservation of salmon and sea trout – species that are fast becoming endangered in Ireland. If action is taken now to reduce drift netting, by sympathetic agreement between all parties, then stocks of salmon and sea trout could dramatically improve in Irish rivers within a decade, and perhaps even within a matter of years, as has been seen in the Tyne and the Tweed with the buying out of the Northumbrian drift netters.

The Atlantic Salmon Trust, also supported by the Fishmongers' Company, has begun fascinating research in May 2005 into the migration routes and distribution of salmon at sea; seeking to establish the effects of offshore fishing, 'by-catch', climate change and food supply. On the Fisheries Research Vessel Scotia, the team developed a method for surveying the upper layers of the sea continuously for fifteen-hour periods and following the movements of individual salmon in a non-invasive way. The Atlantic Salmon Trust is working with the Scottish Executive's Fisheries Research Services Agency and the Norwegian Institute of Marine Research. The next research expedition will take place in August 2006 on board a Norwegian vessel, with high hopes that these new surveying methods will bring major breakthroughs in salmon conservation.

I was interested to find out how climate change might be affecting the fortunes of North Atlantic salmon and spoke to Andrew Wallace, Director of the Association of Salmon Fishery Boards. Andrew explained that there are indeed fundamental shifts occurring at present in ocean temperatures

A truly enormous salmon, but becoming more frequent on the Carron after catch and release began in the mid 1990's. It is hard to imagine that this huge salmon took this tiny fly for any other reason than from a conditioned reflex; a conditioning that began as a salmon parr in this same river, perhaps nine to twelve years before. Allan safely returned the fish and, with luck, he's still out there!

Netted salmon in the mouth of the River Laune, County Kerry, Ireland.

and ocean currents, but that at this stage it is not known how this might affect salmon, or whether increasing trends might help or hinder salmon abundance. It is also not known how changes in ocean currents might affect salmon migration, but with the new methods of surveillance discovered this year on the vessel Scotia the changes can be closely monitored. However, Andrew advised that there are no immediate signals that the ocean temperature and current changes are having an impact on the salmon and sea trout. Other more immediate factors are being identified as affecting salmon abundance and perhaps the most serious is the over-fishing of sand eels, which are caught in thousands of tonnes annually in the North Atlantic. The decimation of sand eel stocks is having a devastating affect on the success rate of breeding pairs of sea birds in Scotland and must therefore also be affecting the fortunes of sea trout and salmon. The Over-fishing of sand eels is truly a disaster for the North Atlantic marine environment and needs to be immediately controlled, with quotas that allow the crucial recovery of sand eel numbers. In terms of over-fishing of wild salmon at sea a major advance was achieved by the North Atlantic Salmon Fund in 2002 when a significant reduction in commercial fishing operations off Greenland and the Faroe Islands was negotiated in the Greenland Conservation Agreement.

On an even brighter note, the most recent reports on the problems of 'acid rain' are showing that evidence of the reduction in emissions of aluminium sulphate into the atmosphere has at last been noted in upland streams and lakes in north west England and south west Scotland, areas worst affected in the past. Counts of aluminium and sulphur in the water have sufficiently reduced to allow regeneration of algae, aquatic insect life and increasing numbers of wild brown trout – bearing considerable hope for the future.

Salar Pursuits, the publisher of this book, is donating 2% of the book sales value (and 1% of all watch sales) to the Atlantic Salmon Trust, currently researching into the survival of salmon at sea and assisting with the restoration of wild salmon and sea trout stocks, and to the Salmon and Trout Association at the Fishmongers' Hall, London – active in many spheres of trout and salmon conservation, but principally in protection of the aquatic environment and aquatic insect life.

Tain Met Station barometric readings on Fishing Days and the times when Salmon were caught.
September 1992

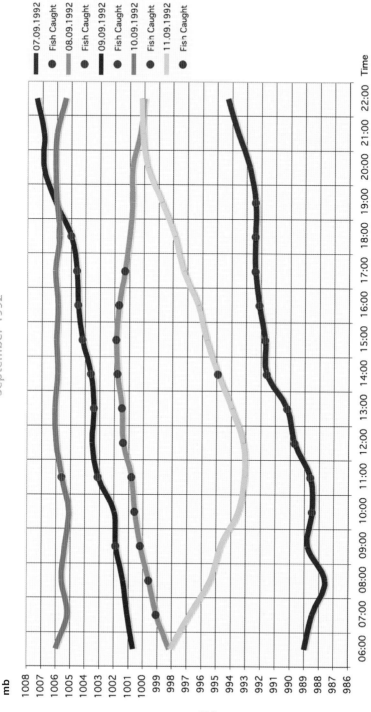

mb

Time

07.09.1992
Fish Caught
08.09.1992
Fish Caught
09.09.1992
Fish Caught
10.09.1992
Fish Caught
11.09.1992
Fish Caught

Tain Met Station

NGR = 2833E 8827N

Altitude = 4 metres

Latitude = 57:82 N Longitude = 03:97 W

Pressure at Mean Sea level (mb)

Time	07.09.1992	Movement	Salmon Caught	08.09.1992	Movement	Salmon Caught
06:00	989.0			998.2		
07:00	988.5	R		999.1	R	07:30
08:00	987.6	F		999.6	R	08:30
09:00	988.8	R		1000.2	R	09:30
10:00	988.5	S	10:30	1000.6	S	10:30
11:00	988.6	S	11:30	1000.8	S	11:30
12:00	989.7	R	12:30	1001.4	R	12:30
13:00	990.2	R	13:30	1001.5	S	13:30
14:00	991.6	R	14:30	1001.8	S	14:30
15:00	991.7	S	15:30	1001.9	S	15:30
16:00	992.1	S	16:30	1001.7	S	16:30
17:00	992.4	S	17:30	1001.3	S	17:30
18:00	992.4	S	18:30	1001.0	S	
19:00	992.4	S	19:30	1000.8	S	
20:00	992.8	S		1000.8	F	
21:00	993.6	R		1000.3		
22:00	994.3			1000.0		

Time	09.09.1992	Movement	Salmon Caught	10.09.1992	Movement	Salmon Caught	11.09.1992	Movement	Salmon Caught
06:00	1000.7			1006.0			998.1		
07:00	1001.1	S		1005.2			996.8		
08:00	1001.4	S		1005.6	S		995.4	F	
09:00	1001.9	R	09:30	1005.4	S		994.7	F	
10:00	1002.0	S		1005.1	S		993.5	F	
11:00	1003.1	R	11:30	1005.6	R	11:30	993.1	S	
12:00	1003.5	S		1006.0	S		993.2	S	
13:00	1003.4	S	13:30	1006.1	S		994.0	R	
14:00	1003.6	R	14:30	1005.9	S		994.9	R	14:30
15:00	1004.2	R	15:30	1006.0	S		995.7	R	
16:00	1004.5	S	16:30	1005.9	S		996.3	R	
17:00	1004.6	S	17:30	1006.1	S		997.3	R	
18:00	1005.0	S	18:30	1005.8	S		997.9	R	
19:00	1006.1	R		1006.0	S		998.8	R	
20:00	1006.9	R		1006.1	S		999.8	R	
21:00	1006.9	S		1006.0	S		1000.1	S	
22:00	1007.4			1005.4			1000.2		

'One must be serious about something if one wants any amusement in life'.

THE IMPORTANCE OF BEING EARNEST
Oscar Wilde

Having concluded my own seven year barometric study, and having looked into the question of 'taking behaviour' using the example of my friends' experiences, I became curious to extend the barometric study to the full independent week of fishing that took place on the Carnaig in September 1992. That is to say to obtain the barometric readings for the full week of the fishing on the Carnaig where I had not been present but for which I had been kindly provided with the catch details by Dan Reynolds, Hugo Remnant and Simon Peck. The fishing results struck me as showing every sign of following the fortunes of a rising and falling barometer. I had already bought the Tain Met station readings of the first two days to examine the 'taking behaviour' already described, but I resolved to spend the last of my dwindling funds on the subsequent three days of fishing to provide, so to speak, an independent corroboration of the findings so far revealed in my own seven year study, in which I had been present on all the fishing days.

The 7th and 8th September 1992 has already been described in relation to the taking behaviour of the salmon and grilse. On Monday the 7th no less than 11 salmon and grilse and one sea trout were caught. Once again, taking a 15 hour potential day's fishing, the barometer rose from 7.00 am until 10.00 pm by 5.8 mb.

On Tuesday the 8th the whole party (the Reynolds, Remnants, Pecks and Mellys) were fishing and caught another 10 salmon and grilse. The barometer was rising less rapidly than the previous day – rising 2.8 mb between 7.00 am and 3.00 pm – more than enough to bring the salmon onto the take, before falling by 1.9mb between 3.00 pm and 10.00 pm. Significantly, although precise timing of the catches were not recorded by the party, Hugo Remnant notes that they stopped fishing at about 2.45 pm. The fish were absolutely fresh and although the strike rate was lower between the rods, it was still a good day's fishing and the fish rose well to the fly, albeit not as enthusiastically as on the 7th. The main activity was in the morning between 10.45 am and 1.45 pm, during which time

Hugo Remnant, as mentioned earlier, caught 5 grilse in quick succession. During this period the barometer rose 1.3 mb.

On Wednesday the 9th another 8 salmon and grilse were caught in a day when the barometer rose by 6.3 mb in the 15 hours between 7.00 am and 10.00 pm.

On Thursday the 10th September the fishing became harder with a day of stable pressure – hovering between 1005.2 mb at 7.00 am and 1005.4 mb at 10.00 pm, and just one salmon was caught.

On Friday the 11th the barometer fell by 3.6 mb in the morning between 7.00 am and midday, then rose by 7 mb in the afternoon from midday to 10.00 pm, during which time, in mid-afternoon, one further salmon was added to a final total of 31 for the week. The party did not fish late on the Friday 11th, finishing early to return to the lodge for Dan's Birthday dinner – if they'd known what the barometer was doing they may have fished on a little later!

It appears the bonanza coincidence of perfect water conditions, a fresh run of fish and a strongly rising barometer at the beginning of the week created conditions for phenomenal fishing which the party have not yet repeated on the Carnaig. The following year they encountered precisely the same perfect water conditions, after a weekend spate, but only caught 9 salmon and grilse in the week, probably indicating that the barometric movements were not as favourable.

It is interesting, therefore, to obtain the barometric pressure readings for a week about which one only heard the unforgettable accounts much later, and to see that, as the final feeding trigger, the rising barometer once again produced the best fishing conditions. The barometric results for this outstanding week's fishing on the Carnaig has fascinated my friends, who were lucky enough to have been there at such a perfect time, and I think we really can say that barometric pressure appears to be one of the final pieces in the jigsaw that provides us with a much fuller understanding of how and why salmon behave the way they do. During this week no salmon or grilse were caught on a falling barometer. When the barometer was rising strongly on the Monday, Tuesday and Wednesday morning, the taking was extremely positive and the fly was taken right to the back of the mouth; and no salmon or grilse were hooked and lost in this period. Once again the barometric pressure movements appear to have defined and directed the behaviour and taking moods of the salmon and grilse.

As already mentioned, I used a Casio Twin Sensor (now up-dated to Triple Sensor) barometric watch to follow the barometric pressure movements while salmon and trout fishing during the seven years of the study. I have not found a better instrument on the market for the purposes of game fishing, and the ability of the watch to give you up-dated pressure readings at the press of a button is crucial.

The Casio Triple Sensor watch will detect barometric pressure changes down to 1mb. Although the study shows that trout, sea trout and salmon are capable of detecting pressure change of as little as 0.5 mb, the accuracy of the Casio watch at 1mb is close enough to the limits of the fish and of the aquatic insect pressure detection to be an excellent indicator of fish behaviour. Air pressure is affected by altitude, just as under water pressure (hydrostatic pressure) is affected by water depth. So in air the pressure will drop by 1mb for every 9 metres (approx 30 feet) of height gained or ascended, and will increase by 1mb for every 9 metres descended.

Since the change in barometric pressure of just 1mb on the watch can indicate whether a hatch of flies is about to begin, or whether the fish are about to come onto the take, it is important to up-date the barometric watch every time you move to a new pool on the river, especially if it is 9m, or more, higher or lower than the previous pool. If you are fishing on a lake (at a constant height) from the bank or in a boat, then updating of the watch (by simply pressing the 'Baro' button on the watch) is still necessary to follow the latest pressure movements.

The Barometer screen on the watch shows a graph of the previous 26 hours of barometric pressure movement, with pressure readings taken at two hourly intervals from 12.00 mid-night. This graph is an exact indicator of the pressure movement over the previous 26 hours only if you are standing at the same height, such as on a lake, or by one stretch of river that does not have height variation along the bank of more than 30 feet (9 metres). If you are moving up and down the bank, then the graph has to be disregarded, and you must rely on the up-dating of the barometer, each time you start at a new pool, and up-dating again (pressing the 'Baro' button on the watch) every time you want to know what the barometer is doing . Is it rising? In which case get ready for a hatch of flies (start fishing a hatching pupae, or an emerging insect) and be ahead of the game for the feeding trout. Hatches of insect can be very short, and to have prior knowledge of what is happening under the water is a real bonus. If you are salmon or sea trout fishing, the same applies – get ready for the fish to come onto the take – concentrate all the harder and fish all the more precisely. A steadily rising barometer is absolutely magic for salmon and sea trout fishing and with a Casio barometric watch you will know when this time has arrived. It may not last long – so make the most of it!

The faster the barometer rises the more the salmon and sea trout seem to like it (since I believe they are responding to this conditioned reflex of feeding on rising aquatic insects as parr and smolts – and aquatic insect hatches are also more prolific when the barometer rises sharply - most particularly for instance after a thunder storm). Thankfully salmon and sea trout can be caught on a stable barometer, and even the odd fresh run fish on a slowly falling barometer, but these are much less ready to come to the fly and are inclined to 'take short', as described earlier. Seeing the barometer falling therefore also tells you why the fish are becoming harder to catch, or even impossible when the barometer is falling relatively quickly. In these conditions the fish simply 'go down', and sinking lines or sink tips with a great deal more perseverance is needed, hoping all the time that the barometer will start rising again.

Eventually the barometer starts to give you better news and you fish again with re-invigorated enthusiasm! The important thing is to fish hardest when the barometer is rising – these are absolutely the purple patches in your fishing week – don't miss a moment of it! The Casio barometric watch has added a brilliant and fascinating new dimension to my game fishing, and I very much recommend it to any and every keen trout and salmon fisher. The added knowledge about the actual behaviour of the fish while you are fishing is absolutely invaluable.

The additional third facility of the watch that constitutes the upgrade to 'Triple Sensor' is the digital compass. This is also useful for the game fisher when wishing to know the direction of the prevailing wind. A shift in wind direction may indicate a barometric pressure change, which can also be determined by the watch, but to know the new direction of the wind can indicate whether a front is forming, or whether it has already passed through, whether the barometer is likely to start rising or whether there may be a period of falling pressure. As mentioned earlier, the centre of Low pressure systems in the northern hemisphere will always be on your left if you have the wind directly to your back. As the wind direction alters it is possible to track the changing centre of the low and establish whether it is moving in a direction that might indicate the oncoming influence of a High pressure system behind it.

As described earlier, these systems generally move eastwards in the northern hemisphere and westwards in the southern hemisphere, and as explained in the next chapter, the system best suited to trout and salmon fishing in Ireland and the British Isles is the High pressure to the south, covering the main part of the Islands and Low to the north, bringing warm, moist westerly winds, rain and a rising barometer. As the High pressure moves eastwards the winds will become southerly and drier, prior to the influence of another Low system from the west and a period of falling barometric pressure.

So knowing from which quarter the wind is blowing is an important asset if you are convinced, as I am, of the significance of barometric pressure in game fishing. Additionally, water temperature is key for salmon fishing, and the Casio Triple Sensor, being fully waterproof, can give you the water temperature, if you didn't already have a thermometer handy. The watch will also give you air temperature and many fishers already appreciate that fishing conditions are better when the air temperature is warmer than the water temperature.

During the summer months when the water temperature is up in the 60's F, the air temperature can quite easily dip below water temperature and this is likely to coincide with the approach of a cold front and, of course, the simultaneous fall in barometric pressure. It is the falling pressure that spoils the fishing conditions not, in itself, the colder air temperature. During the early morning and evening periods (often the best times of the day for fishing), the air temperature can also be cooler than the water temperature, but if the barometer is stable, or better still, rising, then the trout and salmon will still rise to the fly. Sea trout fishing at night follows the fortunes of the barometer, not of air temperature, but once again a sudden fall in air temperature and the onset of increased wind or a shift in wind direction invariably coincides with a fall in barometric pressure, and the sea trout react as negatively to falling pressure as do salmon and trout. All these weather changes can be followed on your barometric watch.

Casio have recognised the potential new demand for their barometric watches from the game fishing sport and have decided to distribute the Triple Sensor watches to the worldwide game fishing market through Salar Pursuits Ltd at PO Box 117, Heathfield, East Sussex TN21 1AF, Tel. +44 (0) 1435 866460. E-mail: info@salarpursuits.co.uk, and online through the web site at www.salarpursuits.co.uk

FOLLOWING PAGES: Traditional trout flies offered by Hardy Bros. in their 1934 catalogue.
By kind permission of Hardy & Greys Ltd, Alnwick.

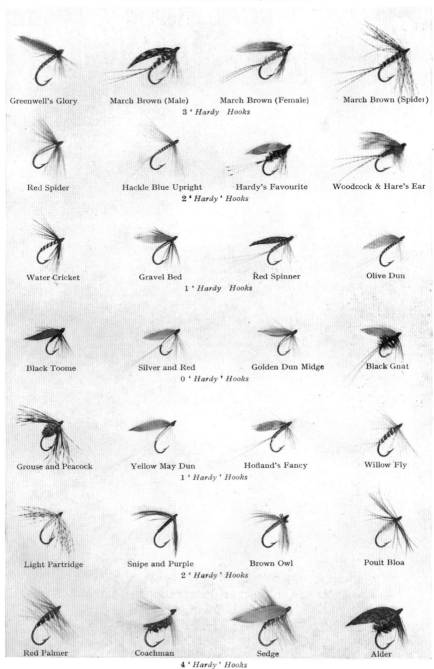

Greenwell's Glory March Brown (Male) March Brown (Female) March Brown (Spider)

3 ' *Hardy Hooks*

Red Spider Hackle Blue Upright Hardy's Favourite Woodcock & Hare's Ear

2 ' *Hardy' Hooks*

Water Cricket Gravel Bed Red Spinner Olive Dun

1 ' *Hardy Hooks*

Black Toome Silver and Red Golden Dun Midge Black Gnat

0 ' *Hardy' Hooks*

Grouse and Peacock Yellow May Dun Hofland's Fancy Willow Fly

1 ' *Hardy' Hooks*

Light Partridge Snipe and Purple Brown Owl Poult Bloa

2 ' *Hardy' Hooks*

Red Palmer Coachman Sedge Alder

4 ' *Hardy' Hooks*

PRIZE MEDAL TROUT FLIES. PLATE 1

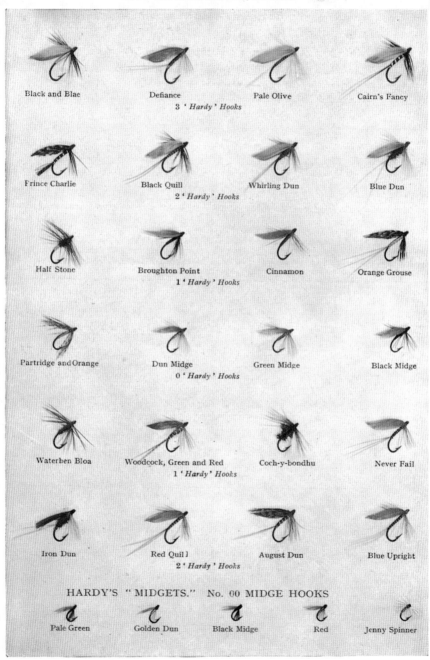

Black and Blae Defiance Pale Olive Cairn's Fancy
3 'Hardy' Hooks

Prince Charlie Black Quill Whirling Dun Blue Dun
2 'Hardy' Hooks

Half Stone Broughton Point Cinnamon Orange Grouse
1 'Hardy' Hooks

Partridge and Orange Dun Midge Green Midge Black Midge
0 'Hardy' Hooks

Waterhen Bloa Woodcock, Green and Red Coch-y-bondhu Never Fail
1 'Hardy' Hooks

Iron Dun Red Quill August Dun Blue Upright
2 'Hardy' Hooks

HARDY'S "MIDGETS." No. 00 MIDGE HOOKS

Pale Green Golden Dun Black Midge Red Jenny Spinner

PRIZE MEDAL TROUT FLIES. PLATE 2

Silver Sedge   Alder   Orange Sedge   Hardy's Favourite

2 'Hardy' Hooks

Wickham's Fancy   Dark Olive   Greenwell's Glory   Blue Quill   Pale Olive

1 'Hardy' Hooks

Gold Ribbed Hare's Ear   Iron Blue A   Cinnamon Quill   Rough Bodied Olive   Red Quill

0 'Hardy' Hooks

Orange Quill   Whitchurch Dun   Ginger Quill   Halford's Hare's Ear   Driffield Dun

00 'Hardy' Hooks

Hackle Curse   Tup's Indispensable   Black Gnat   Little Marryat   Red Tag

000 'Hardy' Hooks

THE " J. W. DUNNE " FLIES

No. 9   No. 11   No. 32   No. 22   No. 20
Olive Dun   Olive Spinner   Brown Ant   Blue Winged Olive   Blue Winged Olive
(Male)   (Male)   Spinner   (Male)
(Male)

" REFRACTA " FLIES

Blue Quill   Red Quill   Olive Quill

1 'Hardy' Hooks

UPRIGHT DOUBLE-WINGED FLOATING TROUT AND GRAYLING FLIES.
PLATE 3

MAY FLIES. PLATE 4

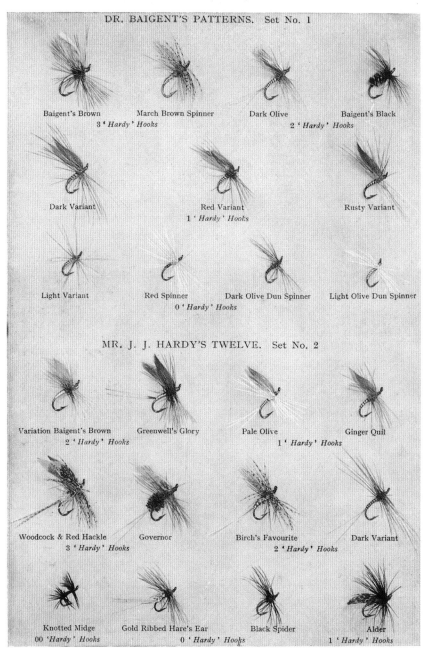

DR. BAIGENT'S PATTERNS. Set No. 1

Baigent's Brown   March Brown Spinner   Dark Olive   Baigent's Black

3 ' Hardy ' Hooks   2 ' Hardy ' Hooks

Dark Variant   Red Variant   Rusty Variant

1 ' Hardy ' Hooks

Light Variant   Red Spinner   Dark Olive Dun Spinner   Light Olive Dun Spinner

0 ' Hardy ' Hooks

MR. J. J. HARDY'S TWELVE. Set No. 2

Variation Baigent's Brown   Greenwell's Glory   Pale Olive   Ginger Quil

2 ' Hardy ' Hooks   1 ' Hardy ' Hooks

Woodcock & Red Hackle   Governor   Birch's Favourite   Dark Variant

3 ' Hardy ' Hooks   2 ' Hardy ' Hooks

Knotted Midge   Gold Ribbed Hare's Ear   Black Spider   Alder

00 ' Hardy ' Hooks   0 ' Hardy ' Hooks   1 ' Hardy ' Hooks

THE " BAIGENT " AND " HARDY " DRY FLIES. PLATE 6

British Patent No. **379343.** THE " RIDE-RITE " DRY FLIES. *See page* **64.**

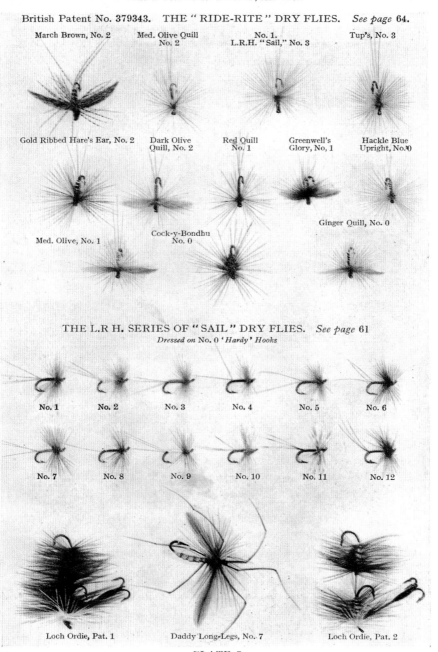

March Brown, No. 2   Med. Olive Quill No. 2   No. 1. L.R.H. "Sail," No. 3   Tup's, No. 3

Gold Ribbed Hare's Ear, No. 2   Dark Olive Quill, No. 2   Red Quill No. 1   Greenwell's Glory, No, 1   Hackle Blue Upright, No. 0

Med. Olive, No. 1   Cock-y-Bondhu No. 0   Ginger Quill, No. 0

THE L.R H. SERIES OF " SAIL " DRY FLIES. *See page* 61
Dressed on No. 0 '*Hardy*' *Hooks*

No. 1   No. 2   No. 3   No. 4   No. 5   No. 6

No. 7   No. 8   No. 9   No. 10   No. 11   No. 12

Loch Ordie, Pat. 1   Daddy Long-Legs, No. 7   Loch Ordie, Pat. 2

PLATE 7

THE " HALFORD " DRY FLIES. PLATE 5
For Nos. 1 to 6, see Plate 4

Chapter Six

Trout fishing and the Evening Rise

'It seems to me that we all look at Nature too much, and live with her too little'
DE PROFUNDIS

Oscar Wilde

The trout, Salmo trutta, is of the same family (Salmonidae) as the salmon and it followed, therefore, that the findings of the thirty-nine day salmon study would also apply to trout fishing. J.H.S Blaxter in **Baroreception**, (Plenum Publishing Corporation, 1978) showed that, using a specially designed pressure tank, physoclists (fish with closed swim bladder, such as sea bass) and physostomes (fish with a pneumatic duct from the swim bladder to the gut, such as trout and salmon) respond to pressure change down to 0.5 mb. In theory, therefore, the response of trout to barometric change should in no way differ from that of salmon.

My father introduced me to trout fishing as a very young lad, and at first it was with a float and a worm in remote Irish loughs, long since cleaned out by poachers. But I wasn't to know that, and nothing in the world was more important than the little red float and the monster fish that was about to grab the wiggly worm that dangled from it. Fishing is all about dreams and I was immediately captivated by the promise of a bite at any moment. As a born optimist with a vivid imagination, I suppose I was always going to be a likely lad for the sport of fishing!

Years later I won a very pleasing bet with my great mountaineering friend, Hamish Laird, when, during a climbing trip in the Highlands of Scotland, I was challenged to catch our supper from the unlikeliest looking Highland peat bog you could ever imagine. To his amazement, with the first two casts, a brace of fat little brown trout were surrendered to us from water that was the exact colour of Bulldog Stout Ale, and they were delicious!

A pleasing moment, as an unlikely supper is drawn from the peaty waters of a west Highland loch, and I win a bet with Hamish Laird.

Fresh trout for supper; and when I told Hamish that his hat and, to a lesser extent, he himself might be featuring in a forthcoming book, he replied "Excellent, I shan't waste a moment in reading it"!

The Hampshire Test. Superlative up-stream dry fly fishing.

A respectable rainbow and an obscenely fat brown trout of 6lbs that rose lazily to my mayfly and came in like a log. The Hampshire Test, June 1991.

Fly fishing for trout in the upper reaches of the Medway, close to home in Kent, was also a happy boy-hood pastime, and then my father discovered the superb local reservoir fishing of Bough Beech, Weir Wood and Bewl Bridge where we spent so many happy days bobbing about in a boat, scoffing thick cheese and pickle sandwiches washed down with Dad's favourite Whitbread ale. We learnt about the tackle needed to find the fish at different depths; the floating, slow sink and fast sink lines, and I became fascinated in the entomology and the flies needed to match the hatch.

Trips to see my Great Aunt and Uncle in Dorset were further enhanced by the opportunity to visit their neighbour, Brigadier Marshall, who was a superb fly tyer and keen fisher on the Dorset Stour. Brigadier Marshall was a wonderful man, with infinite patience and it is to him I owe my passion for fly tying. He taught me how to tie all the classic dry flies and I remember being very proud of my first 'Tups Indispensable'. Breathless with excitement, I was introduced to dry fly fishing on the Dorset Stour and will never forget the 2½lb rainbow that rose to my fly on that first expedition, when I was not more than twelve years old – a lucky boy.

Hunting for wild trout began in earnest after University, when, in the 1980s, we visited the Outer Hebridean Scottish island of South Uist for seven years in a row and explored many of the seventy trout and sea trout lochs that constitute that remote and beautiful fisherman's paradise. The east coast lochs were rocky and peaty, while the west coast lochs were sandy, clear and sometimes brackish. The west coast lochs, facing the Atlantic, are situated inland of the sand dunes amongst grassy pasture and meadows of wild

Francis MacDermot casts a Claret Bumble over the Machair waters of Loch Stilligarry on South Uist. July 1989.

Loch Grogarry amid meadows and wild flowers. One of the prettiest of the Machair lochs on South Uist.

flowers, known as the Machair. The 'Machair' trout, as they are known, of these magnificent lochs are spectacular in shape, colouring and size, and in our experience, extremely difficult to catch!

We fished hard and in all weathers, discovering early on that local knowledge was invaluable and local proverbs ignored at your peril! Once

The distinctive markings of a Machair trout; a stunning but elusive fish, and I was happy to be rewarded when a trusty Grouse and Claret proved irresistible.

again, for Scottish or, for that matter, any UK fishing, the prevailing wind from the west or the south west was a portend of favourable fishing conditions, and one knows now that a dominant High pressure to the south and a weak Low pressure to the north would bring not only westerly winds, but a rising barometer to the shores of the British Isles – perfect for both trout and salmon fishing. Too often, I'm afraid, the Gods were against us on our expeditions to South Uist and I remember many evenings of pulling against stiffening gales, with each of us on an oar, as we battled against easterly winds to make it home to shore and last orders in the pub.

But on the days when the winds were with us (and no doubt the barometer too) we had wonderful fishing with catches of the brown trout in the eastern lochs, the machair trout of the western lochs, such as Stilligarry, Grogarry and Bornish, and sea trout and salmon in the southern lochs of Bharp and Fada. South Uist was a deeply impressionable place that drew us back, year after year.

The eastern end of Loch Bee on the east coast of South Uist. Great brown trout fishing, but you have to keep moving to locate the fish.

Kentra and the Western Isles

Rain racing through the trees
Across the moors to distant hills,
As autumn winds chase after;
Draping greens enthralled in a watery veil.

Beyond the bay to far off islands,
Rise the mountains of age and mystery;
They stand aloof 'gainst a gathering gloom,
As silvery sun is broad and beautiful
over tranquil seas.

A 2½ lb wild brown trout for the author on a blustery day on Loch Bharp. South Uist, August 1988.

Trout feed naturally in their fresh water habitat and although they may migrate within a river and lake system, they essentially live where they are spawned.

In the mid 1970's, Dr Peter Hunt, who is now Director of the Shellfish Association of Gt. Britain, based in the Fishmongers' Hall in London, was working as a Fisheries Scientist for the New Zealand Government. He was studying the potential impact of a hydro-electric scheme on the wild rainbow and brown trout of the Tongariro river system. Every day for seven years Peter was trapping migrant trout that were moving up from Lake Taupo into the Tongariro river system; measuring, weighing, taking scales and returning the fish. Every day, Peter was also recording barometric pressure movements. Peter found that the trout would run the river, moving up-stream, on a falling barometer, ahead of the next rainfall and ahead of the next rise in water level.

So Peter Hunt was recording in the field what John Blaxter was, at the same time, researching in the laboratory. It is possible also that Peter Hunt's findings in New Zealand are relevant to the migrating habits of the salmon, who may also run the fresh-water rivers on a falling barometer, timing their movements to get up-stream ahead of the next flood. So the responsiveness of trout to barometric pressure change appears well proven both empirically and scientifically.

Thanks to the research work of John Blaxter, Peter Fraser, A.Macdonald, S. Cruickshank and M. Schraner over the last thirty years, it is also known that certain invertebrates of the same Arthropod Phylum, namely insects and crustaceans, do also respond to very small changes in barometric pressure – as little as 0.5 mb. The findings are published in **Integration of Hydrostatic Pressure Information by Identified Interneurones in the Crab Carcinus maenas (L.); Long Term Recordings** (Aberdeen University 1997), and, as mentioned already, in **Baroreception** by J.H.S Blaxter, Dunstaffnage Marine Research Laboratory, Scotland, (Plenum Publishing Corp 1978).

Knowing, therefore, that insect larvae would respond to a rise in barometric pressure by rising to the surface from the bed of the lake or river, and assuming that it followed that this would trigger a feeding response from the trout, it was not surprising to find that this scenario would indeed be proven in practice. The three days of trout fishing on the Hampshire Test in May 2003, as already described, produced precisely the results I expected. The fish were quiet and refusing to rise to the artificial fly when the barometer was falling and there was no hatch of natural fly on the water, but when the barometer was rising, the hatch would appear and the trout would start rising.

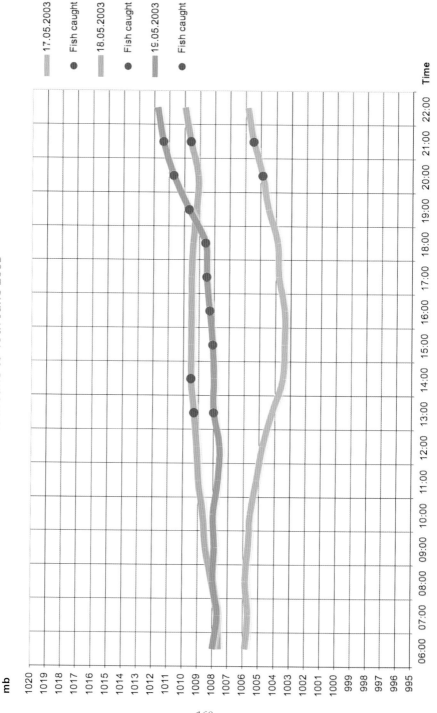

Hurn Met Station barometric readings on Fishing Days and the times when Trout were caught. 17th June to 19th June 2003

Legend:
- 17.05.2003
- Fish caught
- 18.05.2003
- Fish caught
- 1C.05.2003
- Fish caught

Hurn Met Station

NGR = 4117E 978N

Altitude = 10 metres

Latitude = 50:78N Longitude = 01:83W

Pressure at Mean Sea level (mb)

Time	17.05.2003	Movement	Trout Caught	18.05.2003	Movement	Trout Caught	19.05.2003	Movement	Trout Caught
06:00	1005.9			1007.6			1008.0		
07:00	1005.7	S		1007.7	S		1007.7	S	
08:00	1005.9	S		1008.1	S		1008.0	S	
09:00	1005.7	S		1008.5	S		1007.9	S	
10:00	1005.6	S		1008.7	S		1008.0	S	
11:00	1005.2	S		1009.0	S		1007.7	S	
12:00	1004.8	F		1009.1	S		1007.6	S	
13:00	1004.2	F		1009.3	S	13:15	1008.0	S	13:40
14:00	1003.5	F		1009.5	S	14:30	1008.0	S	
15:00	1003.4	S		1009.5	S		1008.1	S	15:25
16:00	1003.4	S		1009.5	S		1008.3	S	16:10
17:00	1003.8	S		1009.5	S		1008.5	S	17:30
18:00	1003.9	S		1009.4	S		1008.6	S	18:20
19:00	1004.5	R		1009.2	S		1009.7	R	19:10
20:00	1004.9	S	20:30	1009.1	S		1010.7	R	20:15
21:00	1005.5	R	21:00	1009.6	R	21:20	1011.4	R	21:35
22:00	1005.9			1010.0			1011.8		

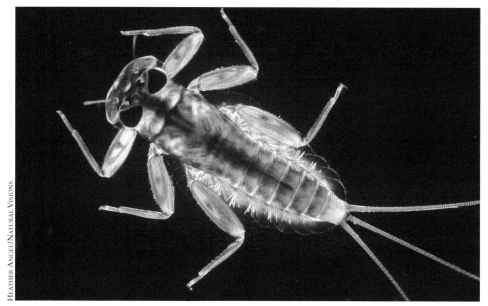

The mayfly nymph, *Rhithrogena semicolorata.*

As explained already, the phenomenon of a rise in barometric pressure every evening as the sun was setting was recorded in the pressure readings at the Hurn Met station, between 6.00 and 10.00 pm; as the surface of the land began to cool, the barometer would rise, and an evening rise of aquatic insects would be stimulated. It has, until now, been generally accepted that the stimulus for the upward movement of aquatic larvae has been the angle of polarised light in the water. But, Blaxter's studies in 1978 showed that arthropods (both sea and freshwater invertebrates, which include aquatic insect larvae) would move towards the light only upon the stimulus of a change in barometric pressure. *'Upward movement in response to increased pressure and downward movement in response to decreased pressure is clearly a depth regulating response. It is usually associated with a geo- or phototaxis, the pressure change only acting as a trigger for movement'.*

So, movement towards the light is well documented, but the trigger for movement being a rise in barometric pressure, although discovered in sea crustaceans and planktonic invertebrates in the studies of Rice(1964), Knight-Jones and Morgan (1966), Flugel (1972),Blaxter (1978) and Macdonald and Fraser (1998), the knowledge has never before been applied to the behaviour of the freshwater aquatic invertebrates that include the insect larvae, nymphs and pupae that are so important to us trout fishers.

The adult mayfly, *Ephemeroptera*, lays her eggs in the water.

The question of whether light alone is the stimulus for vertical migration was something that was studied specifically by Knight-Jones and Morgan in 1966 and Naylor and Atkinson in 1972, but, once again only to the extent of arthropod behaviour in the sea (presumably because of its possible commercial value to the sea fishing industry), but which would also relate to arthropod behaviour in fresh water; *'Diel vertical migration is a widespread phenomenon but it seems to be predominantly directed by responses to light. Light, however, while varying in a regular way to signal dusk and dawn over a 24 hour period, is much less satisfactory than pressure as a depth-sensing device because of the wide ranging turbidity in adjacent areas. It is quite possible for light penetration to vary by over two orders of magnitude in the same area depending on the influence of run-off from the land or turbulence induced by bad weather. The tidal rhythms of inshore invertebrates described by many scientists seem much better candidates for a control by pressure. The organisms are near the surface so that given increments or decrements of depth will give much bigger percentage pressure changes. The tidal areas will be especially subject to changes of turbidity, which would make light an unpredictable stimulus'.*

This certainly rang true with my observations on the riverbank. As mentioned earlier, the insect hatches coincided exclusively with rises in barometric pressure and not with changes in light intensity. The insect activity in the evenings occurred after a warm day, which created the 'Heat Low' that led to the surface cooling as the sun set. The coinciding rise in barometric pressure stimulated the hatch. On cold days the evening change in light intensity would not produce a hatch because there was no 'Heat Low' during the day and no corresponding rise in pressure in the evening – as a result, no Evening Rise.

Similarly, the advent of dawn and the coinciding change in light intensity would not automatically produce a hatch – there needed to be a rise in barometric pressure to bring on the hatch of insects and this could happen at dawn, or at other times during the day and, from my observations, not necessarily coinciding with light intensity, or angle of polarised light.

The receptor mechanisms within organisms for detecting pressure change has been discussed earlier in the book, but Blaxter refers again to gas-containing structures on page 400 of **Baroreception** (1978): *'Baroreceptors containing gas might be expected to have the greatest sensitivity since the volume changes for given pressure changes will be greatest. Amongst the aquatic invertebrates gas-filled structures are found in siphonophores* (including jellyfish), *cephalopods* (marine molluscs, including octopus, squid, cuttlefish) *and aquatic insects* (including nymphs, larvae and pupae) *and in vertebrates in the swimbladders of teleosts* (fish with rayed fins and air bladders) *and the lungs of aquatic reptiles, diving birds and mammals'.*

Peter Fraser, of Aberdeen University, is already earlier quoted, but the work carried out with A.G Macdonald in **The transduction of very small hydrostatic pressures** in 1998 covered the response of aquatic animals where no gas-filled structures were present; *'This paper is concerned with small hydrostatic pressures which appear to be transduced as such, in the absence of obvious macroscopic compressible, and hence deformable, components. Such pressures appear to influence both aquatic animals and tissue cells'. 'A more complex arrangement, consisting of an extra cellular layer, and a membrane with stretch-activated channels complete with cytoskeletal support is thought to account for mechano-transduction in both insects and nematodes'.*

Fraser and Macdonald therefore sought to locate the mechanism for response to barometric pressure and acknowledged that even where there was no obvious gas phase, organisms may still contain *'a small gas pocket which would provide a highly compressible phase, enabling stretch receptors to transduce micro-hydrostatic pressure changes'.* A gas-filled baroreceptor was identified in the water bug Aphelocheirus aestivalis by Thorpe and Crisp (1947); as Blaxter explains: *'This organ is found in shallow depressions in the cuticle covered with backwardly pointing hairs, some hydrofuge and some sensory, overlain by a film of air. When this film is compressed the hydrofuge hairs are pressed down and move the sensory hairs. Adjacent to this structure is a small air sac which may damp out fluctuations of pressure caused by muscle or body movements'.*

It would suggest therefore that aquatic insects possessing the cytoskeleton that forms part of Fraser and Macdonald's studies, and therefore also the aquatic insect larvae that are important to trout fishers, are indeed equipped with the mechanisms to detect the micro changes in barometric pressure that I had observed on the river and certainly down to micro changes of as low as 0.5 mb. Fraser and Macdonald concluded, *'Finally, this review closes with the observation that cells present many structures which might provide differential compression, shear and strain capable of transducing micro-pressures. Microtubules, actin and other cytoskeletal proteins are instructive possibilities because their state of organisation responds to local, mechanical, stresses'.*

Although some of this study material has been covered earlier in the book, it is important for the work of these top researchers to be brought as fully as possible to the attention of the world of game fishing. Most game fishers would be surprised that the aquatic insects that form such a large part of the diet of the young salmon and sea trout (as parr and smolts) and of the brown and rainbow trout throughout the world, do have the ability to detect tiny changes in barometric pressure. I have endeavoured to

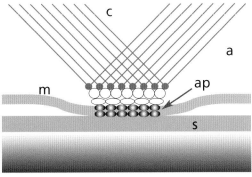

The relationship between the plasma membrane (**m**), cytoskeleton (**c**) and cell substrate (**s**) may undergo a change when the whole system is subjected to micro-pressure. A shear stress might arise in the region of adhesion plaques (**ap**), for example and be transmitted along actin (**a**) fibrils.

explain the importance of this knowledge for salmon and sea trout fishers, and for trout fishers the importance is perhaps even more significant. If, as I believe, aquatic insects ascend to the surface and hatch in response to a rising barometer, then to be able to detect pressure changes on a barometric wristwatch will provide crucial assistance in knowing when the trout are likely to come onto the feed, and what type of fly, wet or dry, to use. Many great books have been written on the aquatic and dry forms of insect that are the quarry of our trout, but two books that came out in the same year, 1981, seem to me to be absolute masterpieces: 'The Complete Book Of Western Hatches' by Rick Hafele and Dave Hughes (Frank Amato Publications, Portland, Oregan, U.S) and 'Caddisflies' by Gary LaFontaine (The Globe Peqot Press, Guilford, Connecticut, U.S).

I was seeking to learn from amongst the most learned and experienced trout fishing entomologists, whether there was any existing empirical evidence of what had been discovered in the laboratory (for marine arthropods), but not yet applied to the world of freshwater arthropods – the aquatic insects. In 'The Complete Book Of Western Hatches', Hughes and Hafele discuss the Mayflies in chapter two and describe emergence (from nymph to adult) as something that can happen at any time of the day, or even night, but the exact time depending on the species, the time of the year, and the weather. Of the blue-winged olive, the Beatis, the emergence is described as the moment when the nymphs release their hold on the substrate of the river bed and float or swim to the surface. The subimago hatches quickly out of the nymphal cuticle in the surface film. The subimagoes molt to imagoes in seven to twelve hours after emergence and then mating flights occur.

Fishing the dawn.

To Morning

O holy virgin! Clad in purest white,
Unlock heav'n's golden gates, and issue forth;
Awake the dawn that sleeps in heaven; let light
Rise from the chambers of the east, and bring
The honied dew that cometh on waking day.
O radiant morning, salute the sun,
Rouz'd like a huntsman to the chase; and, with
Thy buskin'd feet, appear upon our hills.

POETICAL SKETCHES 1783

William Blake

Setting out with a fly rod as the sun rises is a very special experience. The hunting senses are all the more acute, and there is a feeling that perhaps, at this time of the morning, the fish can be taken by surprise! But why should the dawn be any better than other times of the day? My feeling is that trout and salmon do not like bright sun light on the water, particularly if it is shining directly down the pool, and fishing the dawn obviously avoids this. In the half-light the trout certainly appear more emboldened to come out from under the banks or into the shallows of lakes to feed, and this goes also for sea trout, which are easily spooked and best approached at night. For these reasons alone the early morning fishing will be more likely to produce results. There is no automatic rise in barometric pressure in the morning in the way there is in the evening after a warm summer day. However, as described by Hughes and Hafele above, there may still be plenty of insects (in the adult imago stage) on the wing after the hatch of the previous evening, and as they lay eggs on the water, becoming spent spinners, they can stimulate a trout rise. In the forty-five days of barometric data within this book, the barometer is rising by at least 0.5 mb between 7.00 and 8.00 in the evening 40% more often than it does between 7.00 and 8.00 in the morning. The summer time 'Heat Low' created on the warm days will be responsible for this difference, and it is this difference that makes the summer evenings the very best period for trout, sea trout and salmon fishing.

Hughes and Hafele also describe swarms of Beatis that have been observed in late afternoon and evening, and I would suggest that these would be the hatching dun, the subimago, hatching on a rising barometer after the 'Heat Low' of the day. Hughes and Hafele again describe the genus Callibeatis and explain how, prior to emergence the nymphs swim up and down between the surface and the safety of the riverbed, stirring savage feeding by trout. *'Finally the nymphs make a steady, rapid swim to the surface, where the subimago bursts free from the nymphal shuck and is airborne in seconds. Trout often concentrate on the easily captured nymphs, ignoring the escaping duns. Emergence usually occurs in afternoon or early evening, with the duns molting to spinners seven to nine hours later.'* Hughes and Hafele also refer to the Ephemerella, describing their emergence as being most commonly from late afternoon until after dark. Of the Heptageniidae (Red Quill and March Brown), Hughes and Hafele describe the habits: *'After approximately two days the newly emerged subimagoes molt to imagoes. Mating swarms form in late afternoon or evening, often just following the day's emergence'.*

'The Complete book of Western Hatches' covers the emergence and distribution, nymph and adult characteristics, and the fly tying imitations of all the aquatic insects that are the staple diet of the trout of the western

Caddis larva, *Limnophilus flavicornus*, emerges from a case made from cut rush stems.

rivers of the U.S. Not all of the different species of aquatic insect are described as emerging in the late afternoon and early evening, but a clear majority of the species appear to emerge at this time of the day, and emergence at other times of the day may also be as a response to rises in barometric pressure, such as is common after the passing through of a summer rain storm, or weather front.

Water temperatures would appear to play the major role in determining when certain species will mature, stimulating the all important communal metamorphosis to the stage preparatory for emergence – be it as a nymph for the insects with incomplete metamorphosis; Ephemeroptera (Mayflies), Pecoptera (Stoneflies), Odonata (Dragonflies and Damselflies), Hemiptera (Water bugs, including Water-boatman and Backswimmers), or as a pupa for the insects with complete metamorphosis; Trichoptera (Caddisflies), Megaloptera (Alderflies and Dobsonflies), Coleoptera (Beetles) and Diptera (True Flies).

For the different species to survive, the emergent stage must mature at the same time in order to ensure hatching and coincidental mating. Entomologists have observed the ability of aquatic insects to retard or accelerate development in order to synchronise the moment for emergence. Dr Peter Barnard of the London Natural History Museum was persuaded of the idea that the final trigger of synchronised emergence was not a final change in water temperature, or of angle or intensity of light, but actually of a change in barometric pressure – a rise in pressure that signalled a period of improving weather in which to perform the all important mating and laying of eggs.

As mentioned earlier, this barometric influence on freshwater aquatic insects could be observed in a specially constructed barometric chamber, with a two year study carried out by a graduate at the Freshwater Biological Association on Lake Windermere in the Lake District, U.K. It would be

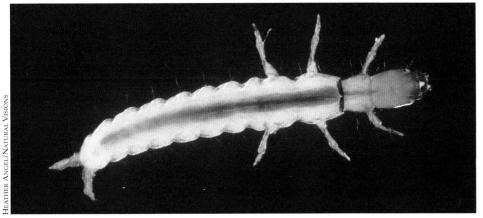

The net spinning caddis larva, *Philopotamus montanus*. The fine lateral hairs on the abdomen, to which Dr Peter Barnard refers as possible pressure receptors, can just be seen.

expensive (£40,000/year) and the conclusions may still be subject to debate, as it is very difficult to perfectly simulate in the laboratory the natural environment of a river or lake. The alternative is to continue amassing the empirical evidence by observing the barometric pressure changes in relation to insect hatches on rivers and lakes all over the world, using accurate digital barometers (as mentioned earlier, I use and recommend the Casio Triple Sensor watch, available from Salar Pursuits Ltd, P.O Box 117, Heathfield, East Sussex TN21 1AF, Tel. +44 (0)1435 866460. E-mail: info@salarpursuits.co.uk, and online through www.salarpursuits.co.uk). Certainly, in respect of my own empirical study to date, the hatches exclusively coincide with a rising barometer.

In Garry LaFontaine's comprehensive book 'Caddisflies', I also looked for evidence that Caddis flies hatched more frequently in the evening in the summer months (indicating a response to the barometer rise after the 'Heat Low'). LaFontaine explains that *'The greatest activity, for both emerging and egg laying, occurs during subdued light, not dark, and triggers major dawn and dusk feeding periods by fish'*. Once again, dawn hatches can occur due to a rising barometer and in this case caddis flies would be present, but over many years of having the pleasure of fishing sedge patterns during prolific caddis hatches in local reservoirs, the evening rise has been the moment – the moment when the sun comes off the water, the land surface cools and the barometer rises. LaFontaine also says: *'Records of flight periods reveal peaks at sunset and sunrise, the peak at sunset the greater of the two'*.

Caddis larva, *Phryganea sp.*, emerging from a case
constructed of dead leaves.

Perhaps the most interesting evidence of Caddis larvae responsiveness to barometric pressure would be LaFontaine's mention of their behaviour in response to a summer thunderstorm, when the barometer will rise rapidly just before the storm breaks: *'In midsummer, when heavy thunderheads roll in at dusk, often a blitz of activity begins just before the storm hits, producing a half-hour or so of spectacular fly-fishing for someone who is ready for it'.*

Do birds, and in particular sea birds, respond to barometric pressure?

If freshwater and marine arthropods respond to a rise in barometric pressure by moving towards the light and rising towards the surface of the water, then it was worth enquiring as to the possibility that sea birds may also respond to pressure, and synchronise their feeding accordingly.

I wondered whether the 'Heat Low' that brought about rising barometric pressures in the evenings on land might also operate in the same way at sea – no reason why not, since the surface of the sea would be affected by sun during the day, albeit less than the land, and this is what creates the on-shore and off-shore breezes; on-shore during the day as the land heats up, and off-shore at night as it rapidly cools. The apparent diurnal movement of marine arthropods was found by Blaxter to be triggered by a rise in barometric pressure. If the barometer would rise over the sea in the summer evenings, in the same way as it did over land, then the migration of marine arthropods towards the sea surface, actually filmed by the recent BBC 'Blue Planet' film crew, could certainly be triggered by the evening rise in barometric pressure, as the sun is setting.

In conversation with an ornithologist and regular visitor to the Shetland Isles in Northern Scotland, I was excited to hear that the sea birds, nesting on the cliffs, would very often begin their feeding in the sea just as the sun started to set; in particular the gannets, guillemots, razorbills and puffins. I mentioned earlier my experience as a young boy visiting the bird sanctuary of Handa, on the north west coast of Scotland, but I wanted to compare notes with a leading ornithologist, Fergus Beeley. Fergus was interested in, and very much aware of, the concept of barometric pressure and the ability of sea birds to respond to pressure changes. Fergus said that the Procellaridae, which include the Albatross and the Fulmar, are known as the tube-noses since they are capable of detecting barometric pressure change in a tube in the top of the beak. The Fulmars of St Kilda, Fergus explained, will head off at dusk to feed; and other sea birds, such as the Manx Shearwater and the Storm Petrels, are able to detect 'Thermo Climes' (areas of ocean where cold and warm waters collide), and arrive at their strongest position incredibly quickly. These are rich feeding grounds at sea, and although it is not yet fully understood how these birds find the Thermo Climes, it is thought they navigate by following the gradient in barometric pressure (that must be caused by the changing temperature of the sea).

In **Baroreception** 1978, John Blaxter refers to a study in the pigeon, Columbia livia, in which Kreithen and Keeton (1974) found that response to barometric pressure went down to about 1mb, equivalent to about 9m in altitude (or 1cm in water). Blaxter noted, *'It is most interesting that the threshold corresponds closely to that of the most sensitive aquatic organisms with a swimbladder'.*

Fergus Beeley pointed out that **physiological evolution in the prey species must, by necessity, evolve at the same time in the predator.** So, Fergus explained, it is possible that fulmars, gannets, razorbills, guillemots and puffins are able to detect barometric pressure and synchronise their feeding to when a rising barometer brings prey to the sea surface, but it is something that needs deeper analysis and further study. Fergus also suggested that swallows, house martins, wagtails and dippers may also be able to detect barometric pressure changes,

Atlantic Puffins may be every bit as sensitive to barometric pressure as the fish on which they prey – in this case sand eels.

and begin feeding on hatching insects just as they emerge (when they may be most vulnerable) on a rising barometer.

Understanding the simple truth of physiological evolution, in the way Fergus Beeley described above, seemed to underpin the whole concept of this barometric study. Salmon, sea trout and trout are able to detect very small changes in barometric pressure because the prey on which they feed are also capable of detecting pressure changes to the same degree, and that these changes in pressure influence the behaviour of the prey, and therefore also the behaviour of the predator.

It appears highly likely that, in following this evolutionary principle, trout and salmon, amongst many other fish species, have developed highly sensitive receptors for detecting barometric change. In **Baroreception** (1978), John Blaxter again describes a behavioural study revealing pressure detection even as low as 0.2 mb: *'Spontaneous behaviour of a different sort was used by McCutcheon (1966) in the pinfish Lagodon rhomboids and sea bass Centropristus striatus and in nine other physoclists (with closed swim bladders) and the goldfish, a physostome (with pneumatic duct from the swimbladder to the gut). All species showed yawning behaviour if the pressure was reduced by 0.2 cm H2O (0.2 mb) for a minute or more. A cyclical swimming activity around a position in the tank to which the fish were adapted was observed when the pressure was changed by +/- 1.0 cm H2O (1 mb) with the first movement being* **downwards** *for a pressure decrease and* **upwards** *for an increase'.* (Bold type is mine).

The question of 'conditioned reflex' is an important element of this barometric study as it supposes that trout, sea trout and salmon can learn that an increase in barometric pressure means that food in the form of insect larvae in freshwater and, for the salmon and sea trout, marine arthropods at sea (including shrimps and prawns) will become available for them; that a rising barometer is ringing the 'dinner gong' that I described earlier. John Blaxter also describes in his paper a study carried out in 1941: *'Thus Dijkgraaff (1941) used an operant conditioning technique with minnows Phoxinus leavis. They were trained to associate food with small changes of pressure and showed clear searching movements after training with pressure changes of only 0.5 – 1.0 cm H2O (0.5 – 1.0 mb)'.* It is hard to imagine that trout, sea trout and salmon are not every bit as conditioned to such a feeding response when pressure changes of a similar degree occur.

I believe the evidence of the study in this book strongly suggests a feeding response based on conditioned reflex to a rising barometer, and as I have mentioned already, I am personally convinced of it. Whether the barometric study within these pages has actually uncovered the Holy Grail of salmon fishing, namely why salmon take a fly in fresh water, will no doubt be a matter of conjecture for some and, as ever, for others a matter of personal preference!

Chapter Seven

A barometer beside the river

'I can believe in anything, provided that it is quite incredible'.

THE PICTURE OF DORIAN GRAY

Oscar Wilde

'The Barometric Breakthrough' may seem a grand title for something most game fishers have thought about, in one way or another, for years. But when those thoughts become a reality and those musings are eventually correlated, then I believe it is something that can be described as a breakthrough.

To a greater or lesser extent, an understanding of the significance of barometric pressure on the fortunes of game fishing has been appreciated for many years, but it was difficult to know the full extent. A good friend and publisher, Nick Oulton, had been giving me some sound advice about the book and therefore knew the subject matter. Nick was talking to a fishing friend of his, Tim Anderson, about the concept of barometric pressure and by shear chance, Tim had just been given an ancient pocket fishing barometer which he kindly lent to Nick to pass on to me. This book was three quarters written when Nick invited the family around for a barbecue, also three quarters of the way through the victorious England versus Australia Ashes Cricket Tour. I expected the lunch to be largely celebrating the fortunes of English cricket when Nick suddenly produced this incredible artefact that had been lent to him by Tim. Here was the original article – a pocket fishing barometer that was obviously pre-plastic era, since it was made of bakelite, and was commercially produced by a company called 'Taylor' for the sport of fishing. With further kind assistance I was able to obtain a 'Taylor' pocket fishing barometer via 'e-bay' complete with original box and instructions, and a second pocket fishing barometer

The *'Taylor Fisherman's Barometer'*, patented in New York, USA in the 1940's and made of bakelite. This one is still in working order.

produced by a company called 'Airguide'. The Taylor fishing barometer was patented in New York, USA in the 1940's, and the Airguide was also made in the US, Chicago and copyrighted in 1978.

The two fishing barometers are almost identical in design, and it appears the Airguide is closely based on the Taylor model. Being the earlier of the two models, and still with the original instructions, I can describe the Taylor fishing barometer in detail. Made out of bakelite in the 1940's or early '50's, the principle of using the barometer to indicate when the fish might be 'biting' was the design emphasis. A dial on the back allows you to set the barometer for the altitude that you are fishing, then the front dial has a face that is split into a *'Low Pressure Zone'* of 28 – 29.9 inches of mercury (948 mb – 1012.5 mb), and a *'High Pressure Zone'* of 29.9 – 31.8 inches of mercury (1012.5 mb – 1077 mb). Within the Low Pressure Zone (coloured yellow) the advice is *'Result Diminishing'*, and within the High Pressure Zone (coloured blue) the advice is *'Results Generally Good'*. In the centre of the glass cover is a movable disk on which there is a black arrow that can be set in line with the current barometric pressure denoted by the red arrow. On a subsequent checking of the barometer, if the red arrow is to the left of the black arrow the advice given on the movable disk is *'Falling – If Continued Fishing Least'* (presumably least good), and if the red arrow is found to be at the right of the black arrow then the advice on the disk is *'Rising – Fishing Best'*. The advice given at the bottom of the face of the barometer is, *'Quick changes, up or down, improve fishing in either zone. Fish are active during sudden pressure changes anywhere on the dial. If Red pointer remains stationary for long periods of time, fish deeper'*.

The instructions for the Taylor Fisherman's Barometer are fascinating. The front page announces *'tells when they're biting'* and the inside instructions begin with the *'Operating Principle'*: *' Atmospheric pressure, a major source of renewing fresh oxygen content of the water, acts as an energising influence on native fish in the same way aerated water is an immediate "shot in the arm" to goldfish in the family bowl. The fisherman's barometer tells when these energising and activating atmospheric pressure gauges are taking place so you can be there when fish are active and in a biting mood'*. Then under *'Proven Accuracy'*: *' In over ten years of research by fisherman in all parts of this country and Canada, their records show that, 94 times out of 100, the most important factor that decides the fate of your day's fishing is the trend of the barometer. Countless records of 3 times a day Barometer readings and the time and amount of the catch made for the corresponding days prove beyond doubt the reliability of the Fisherman's Barometer as a guide to "when they're biting."*

There is advice on *'How To Use It'*, which I described above, and the instructions finish with, *'The Records Show: Fishing is best (1) on a rising high barometer. (2) Rapidly fluctuating readings at any point on the dial may also mean good fishing. Fishing is poorest (1) when the barometer is unusually low or continues to fall steadily; (2) Fishing is poor when readings remain static i.e. the indicating hand doesn't move for a long period; either high or low.'*

There is an amazing amount of common ground between the research behind the Taylor barometer and the research in this book. The fishing is found to improve on a rising barometer and diminish on a falling barometer, and they also describe a success rate in terms of response to barometric pressure of 94%, where the study of this book produces a result of 96% (both amazingly high). My study also found that fishing was less productive on a stable barometer – described as 'poor' in the Taylor instructions.

The fact that fish become particularly active when there are rapidly flutuating changes in pressure was not something revealed in my study, but Allan Donaldson believed that this phenomenon explained fish activity during one week of very changeable weather on the river Carron this year.

The idea that the fish activity is stimulated by increasing oxygen in the water is not something I would subscribe to, as mentioned earlier in the book, since any pool with more or less water turbulence would have different oxygen content and, in theory, fish with differing behaviour. This has never been the case in my experience, and therefore I adhere to the theory that salmon and trout respond to a rising barometric pressure change as a conditioned feeding response, regardless of the oxygen content of the water. However, in the last piece of advice from the Taylor barometer there is another note of common evidence with my own study – if the barometer is stable for long periods of time (to which I would also add, if the barometer is falling), then fish deeper.

My study also found that it did not matter whether the barometer was particularly low, or particularly high, salmon could be caught at both ends of the scale, all that was required was a rising barometer or, failing that, a stable barometer; and in this respect the research for the Taylor barometer seems to have differed.

Before the digital age, barometers were restricted to measuring barometric pressure in inches of mercury, where one inch of mercury is actually equal to 33.86 millibars. The modern digital barometers (such as the Casio Triple Sensor watches) do therefore have the advantage of showing the micro changes of barometric pressure, down to 1mb, that are detected by trout, sea trout and salmon.

I am very grateful for the interest shown by Nick Oulton and Tim Anderson that led to the inclusion of these old fishing barometers in the concluding pages of this book. Few mysterious mountains are climbed at the first attempt. Any breakthrough, no matter how small, is almost always the result of years of accumulated knowledge and experience. I am enormously indebted to the zoologists who have provided the hard evidence for the study work in this book, and in particular, once again, to Dr Peter Barnard, Dr Peter Fraser, Dr John Blaxter and Dr Peter Hunt.

But, first and foremost this is a book for fishers. So, what of the barometric

An evolution in barometric fishing guides; the *'Taylor's fishing guide'* from the 1940's, the *'Airguide'* patented in the US in 1978, the **Casio Twin Sensor** barometric watch of the early 1990's and, on the right, the up-dated **Casio Triple Sensor** barometric watch, photographed earlier in the book.

watches and the fishing results since the conclusion of this study? The seven-year study was only completed in the spring of 2005, and it was in May this year that many of my fishing friends bought the Casio Triple Sensor watches and began following the barometer on their fishing expeditions throughout the summer.

Dan Reynolds was guiding four clients of Roxton Bailey Robinson (a world class fishing and shooting agent) on the river Nadder on Dartmoor at the end of May.

They were all competent fishers, but the morning was dull and overcast with the river unbelievably quiet with hardly a rise. The barometric pressure had been slowly falling all morning. Just before lunch, around midday, the lady whom Dan was guiding hooked and landed a lovely 5 lb trout. Dan checked the watch and the pressure was now stable, it had stopped falling. After an hour of lunch the afternoon was in completely different weather – bright with a slight wind. The pressure rose steadily throughout the afternoon and all four rods had a bonanza, with twenty fish landed in all.

Dan also kindly wrote to me about his expedition, once again with clients of Roxton Bailey Robinson, to hunt partridges at Drynachan near the river Findhorn in NE Scotland. Arriving on Wednesday afternoon a depression came through and on Thursday morning Dan noticed from his Casio watch that the pressure was very low – about 980 mb. After the shooting on Friday, at around 7 pm, Dan bumped into one of the rods who had been fishing the Findhorn. He told Dan that they had caught seven grilse that day, out of a total of twelve for the week. On getting back to the shooting lodge, Dan checked his watch and was delighted to see that it showed, on the pressure display, a classic increase in barometric pressure from bottom left to top right over the previous twenty-four hours!

Michael de Lotbiniere was fishing the Shin in Rosshire, NE Scotland in early September, with Jamie Guise, my father, John, and brother Hamish. Michael reported the party catching salmon only on a stable or rising barometer, and when the barometer was falling they, and the ghillies, tried everything – to no avail.

I was fishing again at Amat on the river Carron, Rosshire at the end of July with my father, Stuart Harris and Kersten Deere. The river was desperately short of water and the difficulties were compounded by a stable barometer throughout the first two days - the 'dinner gong' was not ringing with any great gusto. But, on the third day, the barometer rose in the morning by two millibars, and I managed to catch one grilse at the head of the Long Pool, and rose another fish five times to the skimmed Collie Dog in Bahn pool. While we were having fun in the Bahn pool, Kersten Deere hooked, but sadly lost, two grilse in Sandy's pool. Even in dreadfully low water it proved again that salmon and grilse will come onto the take on a rising barometer.

Hugo Remnant rang from Northumberland to tell me about his morning experience on the North Tyne in August. He had checked his Casio watch as he started into the pool and it read 1020 mb. Halfway down the pool he hooked into a good fish, which turned out to be 11 lb, and on landing it he checked the watch again – 1021 mb, he was amazed and delighted. Later in the Summer Hugo caught the salmon of a lifetime, which by the length and girth of it (he returned the fish) would have weighed 25 lb. Once again, he happily reported that it was caught on a rising barometer!

In early June I had the experience of a lifetime, accepting a business invitation to fish the Namsen river in Norway. In June the river is running high with melt water and it is at this time of the year that the really big salmon run. The fishing is done from a boat in a form known as Harling, with three rods trailing lures at different depths behind the boat. Harling was brought to Norway from Scotland in the late 19th Century and the style has changed very little since then. The skill is entirely with the rower, who uses the boat as a rod, fishing the parts of the river, from side to side, where he believes the fish may be lying. I thoroughly enjoyed the whole experience as it was a heady mixture of coarse fishing, effectively watching the tip of your rods, punting, which was immensely relaxing, and marlin fishing, since at any moment you could be attached to a 40 lb salmon – dragging you and your tiny boat back out to sea!

This was the way my great grandfather David Bett and my great great uncle Fordham Towgood, had fished the Tay as young men at the turn of the 20th Century, and it was fun to give it a go on the Namsen a hundred and five years later! The river was in spate on the first day and rather dirty, but by the end of the second day the river was clearing and at last the barometer began to rise, around 6.00 pm. I was watching the barometer on my wristwatch, of course, and happily announced to the guide that we would shortly catch a salmon. My guide, Egil Aslak Hagerup, had been interested in my theory of barometric pressure and was sufficiently 'on board' to feel a similar zephyr of anticipation as I announced the rising barometer. Even so, he was absolutely astounded when not two minutes later the line of one of the rods went peeling out and we had a salmon on!

This was the first fish that had taken any of Egil's lines in the last 56 hours of rowing (a full week), and I had predicted it within minutes! There was a good bit of luck, of course, for a fish to take so obligingly after I had 'pronounced', but the theatre of it was amusing, and certainly Egil was impressed. As it happened, Egil had a barometric sports watch, which he had never considered using for fishing but which he now set to the barometer feature, and we compared the pressure movements for the next two days of fishing – both watches were perfectly accurate, showing identical pressure movements down to 1 millibar of change. The following day the fishing further improved with the barometer continuing to rise. The water was still quite dirty with detritus from the recent spate, but on the rising barometer four beautiful fresh salmon up to 14 lbs were caught and three were lost.

Egil has kindly kept in touch via e-mail, and he reported an amazing day's fishing two weeks later: *'Norway calling. We're still fishing, and I'm checking my barometer watch continuously, and I'm becoming more and more convinced that you are right; and so are even the fishermen I guide. Today the group who were at the hotel caught almost 50 kilo (110 lbs) of salmon in four hours. The biggest one was 18 kilo (40 lb), and guess what, yep, the barometer rose three millibar during those hours'.*

I can't promise that you'll catch 110 lbs of salmon every time the barometer rises three millibar, but where there are fish in the river and a rising barometer, your next big trout or salmon is only one more cast and a heart-beat away.

Acknowledgements

I would like to thank the following people for their generous assistance with research and advice for this book: Dr Peter Fraser of Aberdeen University Zoology Department, Dr John Blaxter of Dunstaffnage Marine Research Laboratory in Oban, Dr Peter Barnard and Steve Brooks of The Natural History Museum Entomology Department, London, Dr Peter Hunt of The Shellfish Association of Gt. Britain, Fishmonger's Hall, London; The Freshwater Biological Association, Lake Windermere, Cumbria; Andrew Wallace, Director of The Association of Salmon Fishery Boards and Fergus Beeley, leading ornithologist and film producer.

I would also like to acknowledge the following works from which excerpts have been quoted in the book:

'Fish Physiology: Dogfish hair cells sense hydrostatic pressure', Peter J. Fraser and Richard L. Shelmerdine. Department of Zoology, Aberdeen University. Nature, Macmillan Publications 2002.

'Effects of gravity and hydrostatic pressure on angular acceleration coding sensory neurones in the crab and dogfish', Peter J. Fraser, R.L. Shelmerdine, R.F. Findlay, S.F. Cruickshank, A.G. Macdonald, L. Tawse, and G.G. Taylor. Zoology Department and Biochemical Science, Aberdeen University.

'The transduction of very small hydrostatic pressures', A.G. Macdonald and P.J. Fraser. Elsevier, CBP. Nov 1998.

'Integration of Hydrostatic Pressure Information by Identified Interneurones in the Crab Carcinus maenas (L.); Long-Term Recordings', P.J. Fraser, A.G. Macdonald, S.F. Cruickshank and M.P. Schraner. Aberdeen University.

'Baroreception' J.H.S. Blaxter. Dunstaffnage Marine Research Laboratory, Oban, Scotland. Plenum Publishing Corporation, 1978.

'*The Effect Of Hydrostatic Pressure On Fishes*', J.H.S. Blaxter, Dunstaffnage Marine Research Laboratory, Oban. Plenum Publishing Corporation, New York.

'*Adaptation By Cod And Saithe To Pressure Changes*', P.Tytler and J.H.S. Blaxter. Netherlands Journal of Sea Research, 1973.

'*Pressure Discrimination in Teleost Fish*', J.H.S. Blaxter and P. Tytler, Dunstaffnage Marine Research Laboratory, Oban and Biology Department, Stirling University, Scotland.

'*Fly Fishing*', Lord Grey, Dent 1899.

'*Salmon fishing, A Practical Guide*', Hugh Falkus. H.F & G. Witherby Ltd.

'*The Complete Book Of Western Hatches*', Dave Hughes & Rick Hafele. Frank Amato Publications. U.S.

'*Caddisflies*', Gary LaFontaine. The Lyons Press. U.S.

'*When Men and Mountains Meet*', H.W.Tilman. Diadem Books.

'*Scrambles Amongst The Alps*', Edward Whymper. John Murray.

'*The Tale of Mr Jeremy Fisher*', Beatrix Potter. Frederick Warne & Co.

I would also like to thank Hugo Remnant, Dan Reynolds and Simon Peck for the fishing reports from their week on the Carnaig in September 1992, and for their encouragement for this study. Thank you also to Mary Nicholson and Ruth St John for their tireless help with the word processing, and especially for the work on the fishing charts. A huge thank you to Colette for all her support and encouragement while my head was buried in research for the book.

Almost all of the photographs taken of the River Carron and of salmon being returned were taken by Allan Donaldson. Allan Donaldson also tied and photographed the Kyley Shrimp and Collie Dog fly patterns. I am enormously grateful to Allan for his superb photographs and for his support and enthusiasm for the barometric study, without which this book may not have been written.

Bibliography

Lord Grey: *'Fly fishing'*, 1899.

Hugh Falkus: *'Salmon fishing, A Practical Guide'*.

Hugh Falkus: *'Sea Trout Fishing'*.

Stan Headley: *'Trout and Salmon flies of Scotland'*.

Dave Hughes & Rick Hafele; *'The Complete Book of Western Hatches'*.

Garry LaFontaine: *'Caddisflies'*.

Chris Mann & Robert Gillespie: *'Shrimp & Spey Flies For Salmon'*.

James L. Castner:
'Photographic Atlas of Entomology and Guide to Insect Identification'.

John Kennedy: *'70 Lochs. A Guide to Trout Fishing in South Uist'*.

John A. Day & Vincent J. Schaefer:
'Clouds and Weather; The Concise Field Guide to the Atmosphere'.

Jack Meyler: *'Weather To Fish, or Game Fishing and the Elements'*.

Arthur Oglesby: *'Fly Fishing for Salmon and Sea Trout'*.

John Veniard: *'Reservoir and Lake Flies'*.

John Veniard: *'A Further Guide to Fly Dressing'*.

Derek Mills & Neil Graeser: *'The Salmon Rivers of Scotland'*.

Francis Grant: *'Salmon Fly Fishing. The Dynamics Approach'*.

Neil Graeser: *'Advanced Salmon Fishing'*.

W.H. Lawrie: *'Modern Trout Flies'*.

William Currie: *'The River Within, A Life of Fly Fishing'*.

Derek Knowles: *'Salmon on a Dry Fly'*.

Tom Sutcliffe: *'Hunting Trout, Angles and Anecdotes on Trout Fishing'*.

Garth Brooks & Horst Filter:
'The Colt Book on Fly fishing for Warm Water Species in Southern Africa'.

Mike Dawes: *'The Fly Tiers Manual'*.

Dr Richard Shelton: *'The Longshoreman. A Life at the Water's Edge.'*

Andrew Byatt, Alastair Fothergill, Martha Holmes: *'The Blue Planet' BBC film 2001.*